THEY ARE HERE!

How Invasive Species Are Spoiling Our Ecosystems

THEY ARE HERE!

How Invasive Species Are Spoiling Our Ecosystems

ROLAND SMITH

ILLUSTRATED BY
GAVIN SCOTT

HENRY HOLT AND COMPANY
NEW YORK

For all the hardworking ecologists on the front line
of this complicated battle.

Henry Holt and Company, *Publishers since 1866*
Henry Holt® is a registered trademark of Macmillan Publishing Group, LLC
120 Broadway, New York, NY 10271 • mackids.com

Our books may be purchased in bulk for promotional, educational, or
business use. Please contact your local bookseller or the Macmillan Corporate
and Premium Sales Department at (800) 221-7945 ext. 5442 or by e-mail at
MacmillanSpecialMarkets@macmillan.com.

Library of Congress Control Number: 2022920230

First edition, 2023
Designed by Julia Bianchi
Printed in the United States of America by Lakeside Book Company,
Harrisonburg, Virginia

ISBN 978-1-250-76237-5
10 9 8 7 6 5 4 3 2 1

We shall never achieve harmony with the land,
any more than we shall achieve absolute justice or
liberty for people. In these higher aspirations the
important thing is not to achieve but to strive.

–Aldo Leopold, *Round River:*
From the Journals of Aldo Leopold

Life is a miracle beyond our comprehension,
and we should reverence it even where
we have to struggle against it.

–Rachel Carson, *Silent Spring*

We have entered the Anthropocene,
a new geological epoch defined by humanity's
influence on the global environment.

–Daniel C. Esty (editor), *A Better Planet:*
40 Big Ideas for a Sustainable Future

An <u>INVASIVE SPECIES</u> is any kind of living organism that is not native to an ecosystem and causes harm.

The key words in this definition are: *CAUSES HARM.*

A <u>NON-NATIVE SPECIES</u> is any kind of living organism that is not native to an ecosystem and does not cause harm.

The key words in this definition are: *DOES NOT CAUSE HARM,* which is an important distinction.

The Curiosity Itch

had my first experience with an invasive species when I was eleven years old. I was sitting in a theater with a box of popcorn and a soda, not eating, not drinking, wide-eyed, watching a film called *The Day of the Triffids*. It was based on a science-fiction novel of the same title, written in 1951, the year I was born.

A triffid is an invasive plant that arrives on Earth on a meteorite. When the film opens, a triffid plant, the size of a towering sunflower, is innocently growing in a botanical garden in London. A night watchman is sitting at his desk in a greenhouse and laying out his dinner with a colorful meteor shower flashing through the glass surrounding him. It turns out the meteorite shower is bringing millions of triffids to Earth to join the lone triffid in the botanical garden. The first triffid uproots itself and slinks toward the watchman. He hears a scraping noise behind him and gets up to investigate. Bad move: The triffid kills him. Scenes like this happen all over the world. The triffids are determined to eradicate the human race.

To complicate things, anyone who watched the meteor shower, which is almost everyone on Earth, goes blind. Cars run off the roads, airplanes crash, trains derail, ships go aground, and people stumble around in a blind panic, easy victims for the slow, slinking triffids.

The triffids multiply. The few humans who still have their eyesight fight the triffids with bullets, bombs, fire, missiles, and electricity: None of them work. Humans are doomed until two scientists, husband and wife, who live in a lighthouse but don't get along very well, discover that salt water melts triffids. Invasive species problem solved, except that most of the people living on earth are now blind.

I wish all invasive species issues could be dealt with so easily, but in this book you're going to find out that is not the case, because invasive species are everywhere, and they are resilient. There is a good chance you have one or more invasive species in your own backyard.

I have to admit that watching *The Day of the Triffids* scared me. After I left the theater and was walking home, I was leery of every plant I saw, a reaction more ridiculous than the film itself. The fear didn't last long. In fact, it made me more curious about plants and animals, and how they interact.

This curiosity about animals and plants turned into a twenty-year career working with animals in captivity and the wild.

When I was nineteen years old, I was convinced that I was going to become a famous writer. Instead, I got a job as a zookeeper at the Oregon Zoo. I didn't get the job because of my skill with animals. I got the job because the animal keeper foreman, Bill Scott, liked me and had a zookeeper position opening.

On my first day, I checked in with Bill and asked him what he wanted me to do. He said they were shorthanded that day: "The keeper I was going to put you with called in sick. You'll be on your own. Go down to the east paddock and take care of the animals."

I didn't know what a paddock was. I asked, "Where's the east paddock?"

Bill pointed out his office window, down a steep hill, to a long row of animal pens. "The east paddock is on the left. The section to the right is the west paddock. See that tall building?"

I nodded. There was a three-story windowless building looming above a couple dozen one-story buildings.

"That's the giraffe holding area."

I didn't know what a holding area was either.

"The other buildings are the holding areas for the other animals," Bill continued. "That's your string for today."

I didn't know what a string was.

Bill gave me a reassuring smile. "It's not a big deal. You lock the animals into the holding areas and feed them. The diets are written down. Just follow the instructions. While they're eating, go outside and pick up the yards. When they finish eating, let them back into the yards before the public shows up at ten, then clean the holding areas while the animals are locked outside. I'll come down and check on you when I get a chance. Simple."

Bill didn't get a chance to come down and check on me, and it wasn't simple, but I managed to get through the day without killing any animals or having any animals kill me. I learned a lot about shovels, rakes, brooms, squeegees, and wheelbarrows, but I learned virtually nothing about the animals I was caring for.

The curiosity itch was upon me. On my way home from the zoo, I stopped at the library and checked out books about giraffes, bison, tapirs, ostriches, and zebras, which were only some of the animals I had taken care of that day. (This was long before the birth of the Internet.) I then went to my favorite bookstore and bought several books about animals, spending ten times what I had earned at the zoo that day. The next morning, still itching but better armed, I showed up in Bill's office and asked him what "string" he wanted me to work.

"Felines," he said.

I hadn't read a single book about lions, tigers, jaguars, and the twenty other species of cats the zoo kept in its collection. A new itch was born. This pattern went on for years. During the day, I took care of animals, and during the night I scratched my itches.

Eventually, I left the confines of the zoo and started working with animals in the wild. I didn't see any triffids, but I did encounter many non-native and invasive species around the world and in my own backyard. I became curious. I started to itch.

The Dirty Thirty

My working title for this book was *The Dirty Thirty*. I thought the title was clever, but I changed it in the final draft because I thought it was unfair to the animals I was writing about.

The thirty or so invasive species in this book are not dirty in the sense of being bad. They are simply animals and plants trying to survive, but in doing so they are destroying many other plants and animals that we need to keep our ecosystems healthy and diverse.

Invasive species are now the second-most important cause of global **biodiversity** loss after habitat destruction, and the more humans move around the globe, the more invasives spread.

In this book I'm only going to cover a few of the more than 4,300 invasive species we have in the United States, but by the time you finish reading this, you'll have a good understanding of the serious impact these animals and plants are having on ecosystems wherever they are found.

HOW DO INVASIVE SPECIES GET HERE?

In *The Day of the Triffids* the fictional invasive plants arrive on meteorites. An ecologist would call the meteorites *vectors*.

I don't know if you go to school by bus, car, subway, or bicycle, but all four of these modes of transportation are vectors. They transport you from one place to another. Ships, airplanes, and trains are potential vectors. So are the soles of your shoes, the cuffs of your pants, and anything else you wear that might snag a seed and transport it somewhere else. Wind is also a vector for seeds, as are birds and mammals that eat seeds. Water currents are vectors for fish eggs and fish larvae. There are hundreds of vectors capable of transporting organisms from one place to another.

You are probably more familiar with vectors than you think. The recent COVID pandemic is a good example. Viruses are not technically considered invasive species, but how viruses spread has some similarities with how species spread.

The severe acute respiratory syndrome coronavirus 2 (or SARS-CoV-2) was first reported in Wuhan, China. As I write this, no one knows exactly how the virus came into being, but most epidemiologists believe it came from someone eating food that had been contaminated by bats that had the virus.

An unfortunate diner caught the virus. They became a vector. They coughed, sneezed, breathed on, or touched someone. The virus jumped and spread to other people, who then became secondary vectors. Eleven million people live in Wuhan. Some of them left town by car, train, ship, or airplane (secondary vectors), spreading the virus around the world. This led to constant handwashing, face masks, virtual school, travel bans, a shortage of toilet paper and hand sanitizer, no parties, no movie theaters, and many other restrictions to curb the spread of this potentially deadly virus.

This is similar to how invasive species spread around the world, although at a much slower rate than the COVID virus. It sometimes takes years or decades for a non-native species to establish itself in a new ecosystem and become invasive.

Most of the time a non-native species arrives and then disappears as if it were never there. But if it takes hold and becomes an invasive species, getting rid of is difficult, if not impossible.

Biologists who study invasive species talk about the **Tens Rule** or the **Ten Ten Rule**. *One out of ten imported species appear in the wild, and out of those only one out of ten will become established in a new environment.*

7

I know this is a little confusing, but what it means is that only 1 percent of the non-native animals introduced into an ecosystem will become an invasive species. This might seem like exceptionally long odds, but it isn't. In the United States alone, we now have an estimated 50,000 non-native species living here. Of those, approximately 4,300 are considered invasive species, and the vast majority of invasive species scattered around the world have been introduced by humans.

Here are a few concepts you need to understand about the invasive species described in this book.

HOW DOES a NON-NaTIVE SPECIES BECOME an INVASIVE SPECIES?

- It has to grow faster than the native species surrounding it.

- It has to produce a lot of progeny (babies) quickly.

- It has to disperse (spread) widely.

- It has to alter its growth to suit current conditions.

- It has to tolerate a wide range of environmental conditions.

- It has to have the ability to live off a wide range of food types.

- It has to thrive near humans because we are almost everywhere.

- It has probably been involved in prior successful invasions.

- It causes harm to existing native ecosystems.

BIOLOGY and ECOLOGY

Biology is a branch of science that deals with living organisms and their vital processes. It includes botany, conservation, ecology, evolution, genetics, marine biology, microbiology, physiology, zoology, and ecology. Of all these biological branches, I think the one that is most pertinent to the study of invasive species is **ecology**.

Biologists generally study one species in a given environment, like grizzly bears, salmon, honeybees, or elm trees. **Ecologists** study all organisms in a given environment, paying particular attention to how they interact with one another and how these interactions affect the entire ecosystem.

THE BILLION DOLLAR PROBLEM

The cost of controlling invasive species in the United States is about $120 billion a year. We hear the term "billions of dollars" every day in the news, but I think it's good to remind people what a billion dollars is.

One billion dollars is one thousand million dollars. If you stacked up 1 billion $1 bills, the stack would be nearly 68 miles high. So $120 billion would be over 8,000 miles high. Worldwide, the cost of controlling invasive species is over $1 trillion, which would be over 67,000 miles high. No matter how you stack it, the world is spending a lot of money battling invasive species.

Chapter One

Rats

(RaTTUS NORVeGICUS)

I've spent most of my life working with animals. I love them. Well, most of them. I am not fond of rats. Most people aren't. But I admire these invasive rodents because they have managed to invade every continent on Earth except for Antarctica. In fact, as you read this, I bet there is one lurking nearby.

LIVERPOOL, ENGLaND, 1772

Hundreds of ships are anchored offshore or tied to docks at one of the busiest seaports in the world. Merchant ships, scows, warships, skiffs, and schooners dot the murky gray water. Along the shoreline are hotels, taverns, shops, warehouses, restaurants, shipyards, shipping offices, horse-drawn wagons, and thousands of people plying their trade, which is *trade*. What Britain manufactures and grows is shipped, sold, and traded to other countries. What Britain can't grow or manufacture is shipped in from other countries. If you travel to Britain, or travel to another country from Britain, you must board a ship.

Tied to the dock, ready to sail, is a 150-foot merchant ship, which for our purposes we'll call the *Augusta*, but it could be any ship in 1772 from any number of countries. It is bound for New York, 3,471 nautical miles across the Atlantic Ocean. On board are tons of cargo, a ship's captain and officers, forty sailors, ten passengers, and fifty brown rats, commonly known as "Norwegian rats."

Rats love wooden ships. The storage areas, living quarters, and cargo holds belowdecks are dark and dank with hundreds of places for rats to hide and build nests. There is plenty of food for rats to eat aboard, and they don't have to travel far to reach it. On land, rats rarely venture more than 300 feet from their nests to find food, which makes a ship an ideal place for them to live.

During *Augusta*'s five-week voyage, the rats thrived, reproduced, and multiplied. When the ship docked in New York, there were over 200 rats living on it. The passengers and crew disembarked; the cargo was unloaded. The rats had no choice but to disembark because there was no food in their wooden home. They climbed down the thick mooring ropes in the dark of night, skittering across the wharf into alleyways and the basements of buildings. There were a few black rats (also an invasive species) already in the alleys and buildings, but they were no match for the larger and more aggressive brown rats. The black rats that were not killed outright were outcompeted for food and chased from their nests.

The brown rats quickly learned how to avoid the 30,000 people living in the city. There was a lot of garbage in the streets, plenty for the rats to eat. Within a few weeks there were 400 brown rats in New York City. Within a few years there were 500,000 thousand brown rats.

The Norwegian rat (although it is not originally from Norway) is also called the brown rat, common rat, street rat, sewer rat, wharf rat, Parisian rat, Hanover rat. In 1769, it was given its scientific name by the British naturalist John Berkenhout who believed brown rats had arrived in England on Norwegian ships in 1729. The brown rat probably did arrive aboard ships, but long before 1729, and not just on Norwegian ships. The brown rat was native to northern China and spread throughout the world on visiting ships from several different countries.

Rats hang out near people because people have garbage, and rats love leftovers. Like us, rats are **omnivores**. Scientists have done studies on what rats like to eat. Among their favorite foods are scrambled eggs, macaroni and cheese, raw carrots, and cooked corn kernels. Their least-liked foods are raw beets, peaches, and raw celery. But this doesn't mean that rats are picky eaters. When a rat is hungry, it will eat whatever food it can sniff out.

There are 150 million to 175 million rats in the United States, which is roughly 1 rat for every 2 people. Rats don't live much beyond 3 years. And 95 percent die during their first year. If that's the case, why are billions of them still skittering around the world? Babies. Let's do the math. Rats can reproduce when they're 5 weeks old and can have 5 to 6 litters a year with 6 to 8 pups in each litter. This means that a single female can produce up to 48 babies a year, or 144 babies in her lifetime. If 5 percent of these live to be 3 years old (half of these pups will be females), those rats will produce over 500 babies in their lifetime, and on and on.

Rats eat our garbage. What's not to like about that? Unfortunately, rats eat our fresh food supplies as well as our garbage. Because of their voracious appetite, it's estimated that rats destroy about 42 million tons of food around the world every year. In the U.S. alone, the economic cost of rat damage is estimated to be $19 billion a year.

Rats also carry and spread disease. Among the diseases are: hantavirus pulmonary syndrome, hemorrhagic fever with renal syndrome, Lassa fever, leptospirosis, lymphocytic choriomeningitis, Omsk hemorrhagic fever, rat-bite fever, salmonellosis, and the bubonic plague. You can't write about rats without writing about this plague, or the Black Death as it was called in the 14th century, which killed 50 million people in Europe, Africa, and Asia. That wasn't the first outbreak of the plague, and it wasn't the last, but it was the worst. The disease is not caused by rats but by *Yersinia pestis*, a bacillus that lives inside certain fleas.

If an infected flea jumps from a rat to a human and bites them, they may contract the plague and in turn pass it on to other humans by merely coughing on them. In 1350, there were no medications to treat the plague. The plague still lurks in fleas that live on rats, mice, and other rodents, but it's been hundreds of years since the plague has spread to become an epidemic—or a pandemic. There are 7 to 14 reported cases of plague a year in the U.S., and 1,000 to 2,000 worldwide.

When rats aren't eating, they are gnawing. Rats have to gnaw because their front teeth grow throughout their short lives. If they don't gnaw, their incisors could grow as much as 5 inches a year. If a rat doesn't keep its incisors gnawed down, it can't eat and it will starve.

Rats gnaw on just about everything: walls, floors, doors, appliance components, furniture, plumbing, gas lines, cables, and electrical wires. If your cable goes out, it could be a rat. If your house catches fire, it could be from a rat chewing the protective insulation off the wires in your walls.

If a rat can't get into your house for shelter, it might take up residence in your family car. A car is dry, relatively warm, and has plenty of things to gnaw on, or to eat if the car isn't vacuumed out frequently. The eco-friendly wire covering used in many newer cars today is like candy to rats: Instead of being made out of plastic, the covering is made out of soybeans.

Speaking of gnawing and teeth, I should say something about rats biting people, which is rare but does happen. Around 100 rat bites are reported in the U.S. every year. It's thought that there are more rat bites than that, but people are reluctant to admit that their child has been bitten by a rat. I say "child" because most rat-bite victims are children. Most of the bites occur at night while kids are sleeping. Rats target exposed fingers, toes, and faces. Horrible, I know, but the chances of this happening to you, or anyone you know, are just about zero.

People bite rats more often than rats bite people, because people eat rats. Rat meat is eaten in many countries around the world. One reason for this is because rats are plentiful and generally easy to come by, so they make a good source of protein. I've probably eaten rats myself, although unknowingly. A few years ago, I spent a couple of weeks working with Asian elephants in Myanmar (previously called Burma) doing research for a book. The nearest restaurant or grocery store was 100 miles away. The *oozies* (elephant handlers) ate what they could find in the forest. Every night they kindly cooked a meal for me in charcoal-heated woks. The food was good, but they refused to tell me exactly what the mystery meat was. They simply smiled and called it "camp meat." Rat meat is sold in open markets in China. In the Philippines you can buy canned rat meat in grocery stores under the brand name STAR, which is RATS spelled backward.

As much damage as rats have caused in towns and cities

around the world, the havoc they have wreaked on tropical island ecosystems is far worse. Rats arrived on islands the same way they arrived in mainland countries: on ships.

Black rats, Pacific rats, and our old friend the brown rat have invaded nearly every island on earth, eating bird eggs and chicks, turtle eggs and hatchlings, plants, seeds, trees, snails, crabs, reptiles, amphibians, and anything else they can ingest for nourishment. Some rats have even been known to catch and eat live fish. Their need for food has devastated these delicate island ecosystems and led, directly or indirectly, to the extinction of several island plants and animals.

WHAT ARE WE DOING ABOUT THE RAT PROBLEM?

I can usually tell if a city has a rat infestation by visiting a local grocery store. I don't look at the tiled floors for rats scurrying down the aisles, I look up at the signs: *Laundry Detergent, Bread, Spices, Dairy . . . Rat Snap Traps.* Just kidding, rat traps are never advertised. You have to find the section yourself. It's usually next to sponges, mops, bug spray, fly strips, and cockroach traps. How big the section is depends on how big the rat problem is in the area, and this fluctuates from year to year. Even though rat traps are readily available, I think people are reluctant to buy them

because they get embarrassed by the purchase at checkout. *Flour, butter, eggs, sugar . . . I guess you're baking something. Oh, I guess you have rats . . .* No one should be uncomfortable buying rat traps. Chances are your neighbor has rats too—in fact, the rats you have may have migrated from your neighbor's house to your house.

Snap traps work, but they are not the best way to get rid of rats. Rats usually travel along familiar tracks, rarely deviating, and they are leery about anything new or unusual on their pathways. More often than not they'll walk around the trap even if it has been baited with something they like. The snap trap was invented by a British ironmonger named James Henry Atkinson, in 1897. He nicknamed his mousetrap "the little nipper." A rat trap is bigger because rats are seven times larger than mice. I guess that means the rat trap is "the big nipper." There have been variations on Atkinson's design over the years in an attempt to build a better mousetrap, but all snap traps work pretty much the same way. You put a bit of food on the trip plate, pull back the hammer, set the holding bar into the catch, and place the trap along the rat's pathway, careful not to trap your fingers when you set the trap down.

Poison has been the most effective way to get rid of rats, but there are downsides to that. Most rat poisons are put into bait boxes designed specifically to attract rats. Unfortunately, other animals can get into the boxes as well, eat the poison, and die. Predators that eat rats can die from eating poisoned rats. Another problem is that a poisoned rat doesn't die right away. If it lives in your home, it might die inside a wall where you can't reach its body to remove it. Rats don't smell good when they're alive and their smell doesn't improve upon death, at least not for a few weeks.

A relatively new way to kill rats is with dry ice. It's inexpensive and safe for non-targeted animals unless they're living in the burrow with the rat. The process is pretty simple. You find a rat burrow, shovel some dry ice into the opening, follow the dry ice mist to the second opening (rats always have a back door), block that opening, and then the rats suffocate from **carbon monoxide** poisoning.

Rats are social creatures. They live in groups. If you see a single rat, you can bet it's not alone. If you see a rat in the daytime there's probably a rat infestation. Rats are nocturnal. They don't usually risk daytime appearances unless the competition for food is too great at night.

Large rat infestations are taken care of by city exterminators or privately contracted exterminators. These are the men and women on the front lines fighting the unwinnable rat wars. All they can hope for is to reduce the population enough to control it. Everyone can join the fight, though, by keeping garbage in rat-proof containers, and preventing rats from taking up residence in houses and buildings. If you take away a rat's food and shelter it will move away.

I realize that I've been a little rough on rats, but this doesn't diminish my admiration for them. Rats are smart and adaptable. That's why they are so successful in so many ecosystems. They didn't decide to invade the earth like a bunch of triffids. They just jumped aboard ships looking for food and shelter, and then disembarked all over the world, and took advantage of what they found in new lands.

According to Orkin, one of the oldest exterminator companies in the U.S. (established in 1901), the following are the rattiest cities in the U.S. If your city or town is not named here, don't worry, you have rats too.

The Rattiest Cities in the U.S.

1. CHICAGO
2. NEW YORK
3. LOS ANGELES
4. SAN FRANCISCO—OAKLAND
5. WASHINGTON, DC
6. PHILADELPHIA
7. DETROIT
8. BALTIMORE
9. SEATTLE—TACOMA
10. DALLAS—FORT WORTH
11. DENVER
12. MINNEAPOLIS—SAINT PAUL
13. CLEVELAND—AKRON
14. ATLANTA
15. BOSTON
16. HARTFORD—NEW HAVEN
17. PORTLAND, OR
18. MIAMI—FORT LAUDERDALE
19. INDIANAPOLIS
20. HOUSTON
21. MILWAUKEE
22. PITTSBURGH
23. NEW ORLEANS
24. CINCINNATI

25. RICHMOND—PETERSBURG

26. SACRAMENTO—STOCKTON

27. KANSAS CITY

28. CHARLOTTE

29. NORFOLK—PORTSMOUTH
—NEWPORT NEWS

30. BUFFALO

31. COLUMBUS, OH

32. ST. LOUIS

33. RALEIGH—DURHAM

34. GRAND RAPIDS—
KALAMAZOO

35. SAN DIEGO

36. ALBANY—
SCHENECTADY

37. SAN ANTONIO

38. TAMPA—SAINT
PETERSBURG

39. ROCHESTER, NY

40. NASHVILLE

41. CHAMPAIGN—SPRINGFIELD
—DECATUR

42. GREENVILLE—SPARTANBURG

43. MEMPHIS

44. PHOENIX

45. SYRACUSE

46. WEST PALM BEACH

47. ORLANDO—DAYTONA
BEACH

48. MADISON

49. FLINT—SAGINAW

50. GREEN BAY—APPLETON

Chapter Two

Birds of a Feather Invade Together

EUROPEAN STARLING

(STURNUS VULGARIS)

Nay, I'll have a starling shall be taught to speak
Nothing but "Mortimer," and give it him
To keep his anger still in motion.
—*Henry IV*, Part 1, William Shakespeare

In this scene, Hotspur, a sworn enemy of the king, is fantasizing about teaching a starling to say "Mortimer" (the name of another enemy of the king) over and over again to irritate the king. European starlings are fabulous mimics. The composer Mozart bought a starling that learned to sing part of one of his piano concertos. He was very fond of the little bird. When it died after three years, he held an elaborate funeral for it, and wrote a poem for the ceremony, which begins:

Here rests a bird called Starling,
A foolish little Darling.
He was still in his prime
When he ran out of time,
And my sweet little friend
Came to a bitter end,
Creating a terrible smart
Deep in my heart.

The common starling is native to Europe and parts of Asia. Its scientific name, *vulgaris*, means "common." In English the word *vulgar* means coarse, gross, and pretentious. All these words could be used to describe starlings' behavior, but not their appearance. They are very pretty birds, about the size of a robin, with shiny black plumage daintily speckled with white.

The starling invaded the United States in 1890 with the help of Eugene Schieffelin, who was the president of the American Acclimatization Society. The story goes that Mr. Schieffelin, a fan of William Shakespeare, wanted to introduce all the birds mentioned in the Bard's plays to Central Park in New York City. Some people don't believe this was the reason he wanted to release the birds, but what is true is that the Acclimatization Society did release about 60 starlings into the park. Those original birds have swelled to 140 million and are now found from southern Canada and Alaska to Central America. They have also been introduced in New Zealand, Australia, South Africa, Fiji, and several Caribbean islands. From those countries they have migrated to Thailand, Southeast Asia, and New Guinea.

The first acclimatization society was started in 1854 in Paris, and similar like-minded societies spread around the world like an invasive species, reaching the U.S., New Zealand, Australia, and several other countries. The idea behind these societies was well intentioned, but in many cases, disastrous. The members were wildlife and natural history enthusiasts. The New York Acclimatization Society was dedicated to introducing European flora and fauna into North America for both economic and cultural reasons. The group's charter explained its goal was to "introduce non-native animals and plants that might be useful or interesting."

It has certainly been interesting.

The starling is one of the most publicly despised invasive birds in North America for several reasons.

Starlings are noisy and messy. These are minor infractions, but I thought I would mention them because I have experienced these two annoyances myself. We live on a little farm south of Portland, Oregon. Over 30 species of songbirds come to visit every summer. One summer a small flock of starlings showed up and completely disrupted our avian ecosystem. They built nests in the eaves of our freshly painted house. They took over the feeders, chasing all the other birds away. We tried to scare the starlings off, but they wouldn't leave. They dive-bombed us whenever we approached their nests, which was unavoidable because their nests were attached to our house. I thought about removing their nests but was reluctant to do so because I'm not keen on destroying nests with eggs, even if the nests belong to an invasive species. I should have removed them, though, because in July the berries ripened.

We have Himalayan blackberries, another invasive species, growing along the creek that runs through our property. Himalayan blackberries are not from the Himalayas. They originated in Armenia and were intentionally introduced to Europe as a crop plant and spread quickly. The blackberry was brought to the U.S. in 1885 by Luther Burbank. He put it in his seed catalog, naming it the "Himalaya giant" because of the size of the berry. It turns out that starlings love blackberries. I like blackberries too, but not splattered on my house in the form of purple poop.

It's not just in rural areas that starlings cause problems. Huge urban roosts in cities can create problems as well. In 1949, so many starlings landed on the hands of London's iconic clock, Big Ben, that it slowed down by four and a half minutes. They finally got the starlings to leave by using chemical repellents and broadcasting starling alarm calls through speakers, making them fly away in panic.

We got rid of our starlings by changing our roofline, which included blocking off all the potential nesting sites under the eaves. The following year the starlings showed up again, but they didn't stay long enough for blackberry season because there was no easy place for them to build their nests. All the other birds came back, including a pair of western bluebirds, which had never been on the farm before. They would not have taken up residence if the starlings were still there.

Starlings are cavity nesters, meaning they build their nests inside trees, under house eaves, in chimneys, and other sheltered places, as do bluebirds, woodpeckers, chickadees, nuthatches, sapsuckers, and flickers. Starlings are aggressive and territorial and will kick other birds out of cavity-nest sites. There are only so many suitable nest cavities to go around. By overwhelming these limited nest sites, starlings prevent native birds from reproducing.

Even if small birds are lucky enough to avoid accidents, disease, and predation, they don't live long. The exception is the starling. The oldest recorded wild starling in North America was a male that was over 15 years old when he died in Tennessee in 1972. He had been banded in the same state in 1958. He helped produce a lot of chicks in his lifetime. Female starlings can have up to three clutches of 4 to 5 eggs a year. The eggs are incubated by both the male and female, although the male leaves the nest at night to hang out with his friends in a communal roost, some of which have been known to number more than 100,000 birds.

Prior to choosing their night roost, these huge flocks dive and swoop in what are called **murmurations**. You may have seen a murmuration over your house or when you drove by a farm in the evening. As starlings swoop and soar prior to roosting they make wild, free-flowing geometric designs against the dusky sky. As beautiful as these displays are to watch, they can also be dangerous for airplane pilots and passengers.

There are two primary ways that birds can take down an aircraft. One way is by a large bird crashing through the windscreen and either killing or incapacitating the pilot. Another way is for a flock of birds to get sucked into a jet engine, shutting it down. Bird strikes usually occur at low altitudes when an airplane is taking off or landing. This is when aircraft are at their most vulnerable. In the U.S. alone there are 13,000 reported bird strikes a year. Few of these bird strikes cause crashes, but it's estimated that the cost to U.S. aviation alone is $400 million annually. Worldwide, the cost of bird strikes to airlines is around $1.2 billion a year.

The greatest loss of life directly linked to a bird strike was on October 4, 1960. A turboprop airliner flying out of Boston flew through a flock of starlings during takeoff, damaging three of its four engines. The aircraft crashed into Boston Harbor, killing sixty-two people.

Bird strikes aside, the starling is on the top-100 list of the worst invasive species for its role in the decline of native birds and damage to agriculture. In 2008, the U.S. government poisoned, shot, or trapped 1.7 million starlings, the largest number of any nuisance species to be culled. It's estimated that starlings cost the U.S. $800 million in crop loss every year.

EUROPEAN HOUSE SPARROW

(PASSER DOMESTICUS)

Another little invasive bird that has been here so long most people think it's native to the United States is the house sparrow. They may not be as obnoxious as starlings, but they are more numerous, with more than 7 million flying around the U.S. They were brought here from Europe and released in 1851 to eat the larvae of the linden moth, which was destroying trees in New York City. The sparrows succeeded in killing the moths, but it turns out sparrows were primarily seed eaters. They spread across the continent annihilating seeds, food crops, and aggressively kicking native bird species out of their nests, destroying their eggs, and sometimes even building their nests on top of the vacated nests.

There are 1.5 billion sparrows worldwide, and virtually

no hope of eradicating or controlling them. They are here to stay and have been here for a long time. The ancient Egyptians had a hieroglyph for the sparrow: It meant "small" or "bad."

Chapter Three

Slither

(PYTHON BIVITTATUS)

Andrew, a Category 5 hurricane, slammed into South Florida on August 24, 1992, passing directly through the city of Homestead in Miami-Dade County with sustained winds of 165 miles per hour (mph) and gusts as high as 174 mph. In total, Andrew caused over $25 billion in damage, making it the costliest hurricane to hit the state up to that time. It demolished 63,500 houses and buildings and damaged 124,000 others. One of these structures was a Burmese python breeding facility. The snakes slithered out into the raging storm and made their way into the Everglades, a vast, wild area three-quarters the size of Rhode Island.

They weren't alone. Snakes from other damaged houses escaped as well, and not just Burmese pythons. Reticulated pythons, anacondas, ball pythons, boa constrictors, and many others were among the hurricane fugitives.

I like snakes. I worked with them in the zoo for many years. The advantage I had was that I got to leave them at work, although I did know several herp (reptile) keepers who kept pet snakes in their homes.

According to the U.S. *Pet Ownership and Demographics Sourcebook*, there are over a million pet snakes in the U.S., living in some 550,000 households. Inevitably, some of these pets escape into the wild. How many? No one knows. Some snakes escape on their own. Others are set free by their owners when they can't take care of them any longer. There's no doubt that prior to Hurricane Andrew many snakes were intentionally or inadvertently released into the Everglades, but it's thought that the influx of Burmese pythons during the storm established them as one of Florida's worst invasive species.

The Burmese python is native to a large swath of Southeast Asia, not just the country of Burma (now called Myanmar)). The snake is a non-venomous constrictor, meaning it kills its prey by grabbing hold of it with its sharp backward-curving teeth, wraps a coil or two around it, then squeezes until the animal suffocates. Like all snakes, it can't chew, so it swallows its prey whole.

The average length of an adult Burmese python is 16 feet, but they can reach 19 feet. Although a Burmese python can weigh up to a whopping 400 pounds, the average weight of a healthy adult is around 60 to 80 pounds. The 400 pounder was an overfed captive snake. However you measure it, the Burmese python is a big snake, capable of eating a lot of food, although they don't eat often. In the zoo we fed Burmese pythons a couple of times a month or when their behavior indicated they were hungry. In the wild they eat more frequently because they are more active: hunting, seeking shelter, and finding mates.

Female Burmese pythons breed once a year and can lay up to 100 eggs in a clutch. The mom coils around the eggs to protect them from predators. She vibrates, or contracts, her powerful muscles to keep the eggs warm. While she broods the eggs, she doesn't eat or leave the nest. The eggs hatch in 6 to 8 weeks. After they hatch, the 20-inch babies slither away and are on their own.

It's difficult to say how many invasive Burmese pythons are in the Everglades because they're secretive and hard to spot in the dense tangle with their camouflage. Scientists estimate there are 100,000 to 300,000 of these beautiful reptiles living in the Everglades.

Let's take a look at the low number of 100,000 to see what this means. Roughly half of these pythons would be female. Of these 50,000, half would be of breeding age. Let's say that half (25,000) of these have a clutch of up to 100 eggs each. To be conservative let's halve that number of eggs. Now we have 25,000 females each laying 50 eggs a year, which equals 1,250,000 baby pythons. Let's be really conservative and reduce this number by 99 percent because of accidents, disease, or failure to mate. That's still potentially 12,500 new pythons in the Everglades every year and they can live into their twenties.

Burmese pythons have no natural predators in the Everglades with the exception of alligators (and on rare occasions Burmese pythons have been known to eat small alligators).

By 2011, researchers identified up to 25 species of birds in the stomach remains of 85 eradicated Burmese pythons found in Everglades National Park.

In 2012, 20 years after Hurricane Andrew, in areas where the Burmese pythons were well established in the Everglades, researchers discovered that foxes and rabbits had disappeared. Sightings of raccoons are down by 99.3 percent, opossums by 98.9 percent, and white-tailed deer by 94.1 percent. Is this decline due to the presence of the Burmese python? Scientists believe it is. What are they doing about it?

Pet Burmese pythons have been banned in Florida and other southern states. Violators can be imprisoned or fined $500,000 if convicted. This law has helped prevent new Burmese pythons from being released into the wild, but it hasn't solved the python problem in the Everglades. It's too late to eradicate them. As with the brown rat and other invasive species, the most we can hope for is to control them.

In 2013, Florida held its first "Python Challenge": open

to anyone who wants to participate. The monthlong contest offered incentives such as prizes for the longest and the greatest number of captured pythons. The purpose of the challenge was to raise awareness about the invasive species, increase participation from the public, and to remove as many pythons as possible from the Everglades. At the end of the contest, 68 pythons were taken. That's not very many, but it was a start. The Python Challenge became a yearly event. (About 200 snakes were taken in 2021.) It also led to the creation, in 2017, of the state-sanctioned Python Elimination Program, managed by the South Florida Water Management Governing Board and the Florida Fish and Wildlife Conservation Commission; the program continues today.

Python hunters are paid the Florida minimum hourly wage up to ten hours daily. Time spent searching for pythons is verified by a GPS tracking app on the bounty hunter's cell phone. They are paid an extra $50 for each python measuring up to 4 feet long, an extra $25 for each foot measured above 4 feet, and an additional $200 for eliminating a python found guarding a nest with eggs.

By 2020, the bounty hunters had brought in 5,000 invasive snakes, which is around 36,000 pounds of pythons. An infinitesimal drop in the ecological bucket, but not without significance. This small catch has saved tens of thousands of native species living in the Everglades.

A recent innovation for finding the elusive python is mosquitoes. It turns out that mosquitoes like python blood. Mosquitoes don't travel far from where they hatch. Scientists are analyzing the insects' blood for the presence of python DNA in order to narrow down the search areas, to help the python hunters find the snakes

Surprisingly, the Burmese python has been designated a threatened species in Southeast Asia. A threatened species is defined as: "Any species that is likely to become an endangered species within the foreseeable future throughout all or a significant portion of its range." They are being slaughtered and skinned to make boots, purses, and fashionable vests and coats. They are also being eaten, especially in China. Some of their body parts are used in folk medicines.

THE BROWN TREE SNAKE

(BOIGA IRREGULARIS)

I can't leave this section without mentioning the invasive brown tree snake. You probably won't find it slithering in the continental U.S. (except maybe in Texas, where a few have been spotted over the years), but you'll see plenty of them on the island of Guam, which is an unincorporated territory of the United States.

The brown tree snake, also known as the brown catsnake because of its catlike eyes, is native to the eastern and northern coasts of Australia, eastern Indonesia,

Papua New Guinea, and many islands in northwestern Melanesia. It is a slender, mildly venomous snake that can reach lengths of 3 to 6 feet. I say "mildly venomous" because the brown tree snake doesn't inject venom through its front fangs like a rattlesnake or a cobra does. Instead, it has two grooved venomous fangs at the rear of its mouth. Because of where the fangs are located it is difficult for them to get venom into humans.

Brown tree snakes are fast, aggressive, and deadly to small mammals and birds. Like most snakes, they are nocturnal, preferring to curl up somewhere during the day and waiting to hunt at night. They are also arboreal, meaning they spend a lot of time slithering through the branches of the trees where their prey lives. Their light, agile bodies are perfect for this type of hunting.

The brown tree snake was first spotted in Guam in 1953 and was thought to have been introduced near the end of World War II when the island became an important U.S. military base. The snakes arrived as stowaways in the cargo holds of ships and airplanes and quickly established themselves on the island.

It's estimated that there are now between 8 and 20 brown tree snakes on every acre in Guam. This population density is one of the highest snake densities ever recorded anywhere in the world.

My family and I live on 6 acres south of Portland, Oregon. If our farm was in Guam, we would have between 48 and 120 brown tree snakes living on our property, which would be devastating for the songbirds we enjoy watching. Brown tree snakes are capable of eating up to 70 percent of their body mass every day.

Before the introduction of the brown tree snake, Guam had 12 species of native forest birds. Today 10 of those are extinct, and the other 2 species each have fewer than 200 individuals. This has had a negative impact on the forest because birds pollinate plants and trees and spread seeds. It's thought that 60 to 70 percent of tree seeds in Guam are dispersed by birds.

The U.S. spends about $3.5 million a year fighting Guam's brown tree snake invasion. Half of this money is spent on trapping and killing the snakes. The other half is spent on stopping the snakes from getting off the island and spreading onto other islands. This is done with snake-sniffing dogs. Before airplanes and ships leave Guam, canine inspectors sniff out cargo areas and wheel wells for reptilian hitchhikers

Chapter Four

Skitter

I have visited Florida as an author and a tourist, and also as a research biologist to release red wolves back into the wild. I've been there at least a hundred times. I love Florida. Unfortunately, invasive species love Florida too. It is home to more non-native species of reptile than anywhere else in the world. In part, this is due to the state's subtropical climate. Cold snaps are rare in Florida and don't last long, which is perfect for reptiles, because long periods of cold can kill them. There are miles of undeveloped land for reptiles to hide in and hunt in, including the 1.5 million-acre Everglades National Park, the largest tropical wilderness in the United States, and the largest wilderness area of any kind east of the Mississippi River.

The Florida Fish and Wildlife Conservation Commission has identified 50 types of non-native turtles, crocodilians, snakes, and lizards basking, swimming, slithering, and skittering around the state. Most of these reptiles and amphibians were initially imported into the U.S. via Florida for the pet trade.

There is nothing wrong with having a pet snake, turtle, or lizard. They all have their charms, but you need to be a responsible pet owner. Part of this is making sure your pet doesn't escape. Even worse is setting it free on purpose. People get tired of their pets, their living situation changes, the pet grows too big, the pet becomes too expensive to feed . . . there are a lot of reasons for wanting to get rid of a pet. But releasing it into the wild is not the solution. Chances are your former pet will die from starvation, accident, or predation soon after it's free. That's bad, but what's worse is that your pet might find a mate, reproduce, and establish a harmful invasive species in the wild.

THE BLACK AND WHITE TEGU

(Salvator Merianae)

The black and white tegu, native to South America, is the largest of the tegu lizards. In Venezuela, the black and white tegu is known as *el lobo pollero*, or "the chicken wolf" because it raids chicken coops, devouring eggs and chicks. It is also sometimes called "the giant tegu," or "the huge tegu," and with good reason. It can grow to over 4 feet in length and weigh as much as 15 pounds. That cute little lizard you bought at the pet store can quickly grow into a big problem. It can reach 75 percent of its final growth within a year.

Tegus are omnivorous. They eat insects, spiders, snails, fruits, seeds, small rodents, birds, bird eggs, alligator eggs, turtle eggs, and dog and cat food if you leave it on your porch. They are voracious. In the zoo we fed chicken eggs to tegus on a regular basis, and I can attest to the fact that they love eggs as much I love scoops of ice cream.

Tegus are capable of running at high speeds and can run on their hind legs, or **bipedally**, for short distances. When the temperature drops in late autumn, tegus can go into a state called **brumation**, the cold-blooded version of hibernation that some warm-blooded animals use to conserve energy during cold periods. Tegus wake up from this sleeplike state briefly to drink water, but they don't hunt or eat during brumation. I mention this because this ability allows them to live in cooler climates north of Florida like South Carolina and Georgia.

The threatened gopher tortoise is the state reptile of both Florida and Georgia. Gopher tortoises spend most of their time in the deep burrows they dig, sheltering from the summer heat, the winter cold, and predators. The invasive tegus not only eat tortoise eggs, but also take over tortoises' homes by booting them out of their burrows.

Tegus are **diurnal**, active during the day, and spend most of their time on or near the ground. They are not good climbers. They can lay 35 eggs a year. The hatchlings are about 1 foot long when they emerge from their leathery eggs. Tegus live for 15 to 20 years.

Invasive species biologists have no idea how many tegus are skittering around Florida, but it's thought to be in the thousands. What's also worrisome is that in South America, tegus are heavily hunted for their skin, and yet there are still plenty of them living in their native range. Between 2000 and 2010, nearly 80,000 live tegus were imported to the U.S. to be sold as pets. Most of these did not escape, but it takes only one breeding pair to produce hundreds of baby tegus in the wild.

Tegus are not the only lizards that have invaded Florida. There are 19 different invasive iguana species, 6 invasive whiptail and wall species, 12 gecko species, 1 monitor species, and 36 other lizard species that have been observed in the wild, but are not yet numerous enough to be designated as invasive.

NILE MONITOR

(VARANUS NILOTICUS)

The Nile monitor is Florida's largest invasive lizard. This 6-foot giant is native to the Nile River delta in North Africa and ranges all the way down to South Africa. Every year around 500,000 Nile monitor skins are shipped around the world to be made into shoes, bags, and accessories. Another 10,000 monitors are exported live for the pet trade. Not surprisingly, some of these have ended up in Florida, escaped, and established themselves in several counties. Because Nile monitors like to be near water, it's thought that South Florida's extensive canal system may be helping them spread. There are now three permanent breeding populations in the state.

Nile monitors grow quickly, breed at an early age, and can lay up to 60 eggs in a single clutch. They are carnivores and eat pretty much anything they can catch or find—eggs, birds, fish, small mammals, carrion—and have even been known to attack cats and dogs. They are drawn to the same waterfront properties that Floridians love.

THE GREEN IGUANA

(IGUANA IGUANA)

There is an alphabet of non-native lizards living in Florida: agama, anole, basilisk, butterfly, chameleon, collared, curly-tailed, dragon, garden, horned, iguana, lava, and probably a few others that have not been reported. The majority of these lizards eat insects, which is good because there are a lot of bugs in Florida. The others are **herbivores**, meaning they eat plants. The most common, or noticeable plant eater is the iguana, of which there are 6 species: the Mexican spiny-tail iguana, rhinoceros iguana, Cuban rock iguana, mop-headed iguana, and the green iguana. Of these, the one you're most likely to see if you're in Florida is the green iguana. But don't be fooled, the green iguana is not always green. It comes in a kaleidoscope of colors. You'll see them in blue, black, brown, orange, red, green, and every shade in between. The color depends on where they're from in their native range from Mexico to South America.

It's thought that the first batch of green iguanas arrived in Florida in the mid-1960s as stowaways aboard ships carrying fruit from South America. Over the years, this small population exploded with the accidental (or intentional) release of pet iguanas. In 1995 alone, 800,000 green iguanas were imported into the U.S. Most of these came from captive breeding facilities for the pet and leather trade in Honduras, Colombia, El Salvador, and Panama.

No one knows how many invasive iguanas are in Florida, but there are certainly tens of thousands. They can reach 6 feet in length, most of which is their whippy tail. They can weigh up to 20 pounds, but the average weight is around 9 pounds. Females lay 20 to 70 eggs a year. The hatchlings emerge from the nest after 10 to 15 weeks of incubation. Juveniles stay in sibling groups for the first year of their lives and can live to be 15 to 20 years old.

Green iguanas are active during the day and are agile climbers. They have been known to fall out of trees from a height of 50 feet without harm. In January 2008, a number of iguanas fell out of trees during a cold snap (unusual for South Florida). "The Frozen Iguana Shower" as it was called, was caused by the iguanas losing their grip on branches when they got too chilled. Most of the iguanas were able to skitter away after they warmed up. Iguana showers occurred again in January 2010, January 2018, and December 2020, after prolonged cold fronts again hit South Florida.

Iguanas are good swimmers. They swim underwater with their limbs dangling at their sides, using their powerful tails to propel them forward. They are also well-known burrowers, digging holes up to 6 feet deep and 7 inches in diameter. They burrow into canals, levees, and dikes along seawalls, as well as under houses, sidewalks, commercial buildings, and roads, causing millions of dollars of damage.

Iguanas eat almost every type of plant they can find. This is a nuisance for gardeners and can be deadly for native animals that depend on certain plants to survive. An example is the endangered and beautiful Miami blue butterfly. The Miami blue lays eggs on, and eats, the gray nickerbean plant, which iguanas love to eat too. The more nickerbean plants the iguana eats, the fewer places the Miami blue has to lay its eggs. As the nickerbean plant disappears, so does the Miami blue. This trickle-down effect is how nature works: If an animal or plant is removed from or introduced to an ecosystem, every other animal or plant in that ecosystem is affected, for better or for worse.

These lizards are not leaving Florida anytime soon, but state officials have enacted, or are trying to enact, several laws to curb the influx of new iguanas and other invasive reptiles into the state.

The Florida Fish and Wildlife Conservation Commission declared that homeowners do not need a permit to kill iguanas on their own property, and encourages them to do so whenever possible, as long as they kill the iguanas humanely. Unfortunately, they didn't tell people how to "humanely" kill an iguana. This open season on iguanas has caused a lot of controversy among Floridians, reptile enthusiasts, and the Humane Society of the United States. These groups recognize that iguanas are a problem, but they do not endorse the wholesale slaughter of these interesting reptiles.

WHAT IS FLORIDA DOING ABOUT ITS INVASIVE REPTILES?

As noted earlier, Floridians are having python derbies to kill the invasive Burmese python, with little complaint from the general public. But snake killing goes beyond this. Any Florida resident with a $26 hunting license can kill pythons on four areas of state-managed lands near the Florida Everglades. This permit allows hunters to kill non-native snakes and lizards including Indian and African rock pythons, reticulated pythons, scrub pythons, green anacondas, and Nile monitor lizards. Hunters are free to do whatever they wish with the reptiles' skin and meat.

Another ordinance Florida wildlife officials are trying to enact, although without much success so far, is the prohibition of purchasing, owning, and/or breeding all species of tegus, iguanas, and pythons without a limited license, which is usually given only to zoos and educational institutions. This proposed law has reptile enthusiasts, breeders, importers/exporters, and pet stores up in arms. They want to know why they should be punished for something irresponsible pet owners have caused. Another argument they make is that if officials want to ban reptiles, they should first ban domestic cats, which is a good segue to the next invasive species.

Chapter Five

Catastrophe

(feLIS CaTUS)

In 1894, on a tiny island off the coast of New Zealand, there lived a lighthouse keeper named David Lyall and his pregnant cat, Tibbles. On the island with them was a tiny flightless bird called the Stephens Island wren, which was found nowhere else in the world. Prior to the arrival of David and Tibbles, the wren had no predators on the island. Mr. Lyall was an amateur naturalist. When he wasn't tending the lighthouse, he was documenting the unique birds living on the island and preserving their skins and bones for later study. Many of the dead birds were brought to him by Tibbles, who was allowed to run free on the island, as were her offspring. By 1895, the Stephens Island wren was extinct. The only evidence we have of the bird's existence is the preserved specimens that Mr. Lyall gave or sold to museums. In 1899, the new lighthouse keeper removed more than 100 feral cats in a period of 10 months. In 1925, the island was finally cleared of cats, but it was too late for the little flightless wren. (The above incident is reported in more detail in Dr. Peter P. Marra's and Chris Santella's well-documented and somewhat controversial book *Cat Wars*.)

I'm not a cat hater—in fact, I'm just the opposite. For many years I was the senior feline keeper at the Oregon Zoo. I lived and breathed cats and have fond memories of every cat I had the pleasure and privilege to work with. But when I see an outdoor cat, I see dead birds. I can't help it. The number of birds cats kill every year is shocking.

People have been keeping cats (or cats have been keeping people) for nearly 10,000 years.

No one knows for certain when cats came to the U.S., but it's thought to have been around 500 years ago, when they were brought aboard ships to control rodents. These control measures didn't get rid of the rats, but it certainly helped spread cats around the world.

In the U.S. there are an estimated 95 million cats living in 46 million homes, and 60 million to 80 million feral (wild domestic) cats. This means there is one cat for every two to three people living in the U.S. Predation by domestic cats is the number-one direct, human-caused threat to birds in the United States and Canada.

This is a conservative estimate. It could be as high as 4 billion birds. The average number of small mammals killed every year by domestic cats is 12.3 billion. The number of amphibians cats kill is 95 million to 299 million. For reptiles, the number is 258 million to 822 million. The scientific papers claiming these staggering numbers were **peer reviewed**. This means that other scientists reviewed the methods of the studies to make sure the numbers were largely correct.

Depending on who you talk to, there are between 40 and 71 domestic cat breeds. The Cat Fanciers' Association recognizes 42 breeds, while the International Cat Association recognizes 71 breeds. Regardless of the breed, all domestic cats can and do kill birds, reptiles, and amphibians. Domestic cats are highly evolved predators that are hardwired to hunt. Their opportunity to hunt depends on their living circumstances.

For this book I'll define a *house cat* as an owned domestic cat that stays inside all the time; a *free-ranging cat* as an owned domestic cat that spends some time outside; a *stray cat* as a homeless cat that hangs around houses and neighborhoods; a *barn cat* as an owned domestic cat that might be fed by humans once in a while, but whose primary role is to take care of pests like rodents outside the house; and finally, a *feral cat* as a domestic cat that lives in a wild state and has very little to do with humans.

Several years ago, I had an ecological catastrophe of my own making. I mention it so you'll know that even a well-informed research biologist can make mistakes. One of our nieces brought us two stray cats. We already had horses, cows, goats, and dogs, so the last thing we needed was a couple of cats, but we said we would put them in our barn so they could have a go at the mice, of which there were many. The cats did a good job on the mice.

In the spring we leave our barn doors open so the returning swallows can nest inside. They make quite a mess, but it's worth it because we like to watch the swooping, acrobatic swallows catching insects in the evenings.

Unfortunately, the swallows' arrival was like Uber Eats for our barn cats. I'm not sure how many swallows were swallowed, but one would have been too many. We haven't had a cat on the farm since the two strays left.

Mistakes like this are repeated millions of times a day all over the world, to the detriment of birds and other small animals.

Cats can have kittens when they are 5 months old. They can give birth 3 to 5 times a year. The average litter size is 4 kittens. The average lifespan for a cat is 15 years. This means a cat can produce several hundred kittens in her lifetime. The obvious solution to this population explosion is to spay or neuter your cat. But this would not solve the problem of cats killing birds.

Stray and feral cats kill three times as many animals as owned cats. These cats aren't to be blamed: Like all animals, they are just trying to survive. Some stray cats are semi-owned, meaning that kindhearted people put food out for the cats because they feel sorry for them. It's hard not to. Just as cats are hardwired to hunt, most people are hardwired to help animals. But I think this is a mistake, just like the one I made with the swallows. We fed the barn cats, but they still killed swallows. It's their nature. Outdoor domestic cats have been implicated in at least 33 extinctions around the world . . . so far.

People are trying to stem the cat invasion, but the programs haven't been very effective. There are trap-neuter-return programs, trap-neuter-adopt programs, and trap-euthanize programs.

The trap-neuter-return program doesn't work because spayed and neutered cats still kill small wild animals. The catch rate for unowned cats is only about 2 percent. With this low number, the program can't keep up with the number of cats that are abandoned.

The trap-neuter-adopt program has potential as long as people keep their adopted cats inside, which most people aren't willing to do.

We have to do something to protect our native birds, whose

population has dropped 29 percent since 1970. I'm not saying that cats are solely responsible for this alarming decline, but they have certainly contributed to it. Bird populations are also decreasing because of habitat loss, global climate change, invasive-bird competition, and natural calamities like forest fires, floods, droughts, and freezes.

Not surprisingly, the trap-euthanize program is not popular in the U.S. Cats are fascinating, beautiful, and often cuddly. People generally don't want to see them killed, but the concept isn't as radical as it sounds. Australia has killed millions of feral cats in the outback in order to protect their native birds. So has New Zealand. American shelters put down more than 1.4 million cats a year. That seems like a lot, but it's barely making a difference because there are still millions of feral, stray, and free-ranging cats hunting outside.

Aside from the predation problem, cats can also carry and spread disease to humans. This is called **zoonosis**. One of the diseases cats carry and pass to humans and other animals comes from a parasite called *Toxoplasma gondii*. It lives in cat poop. At the zoo we didn't allow pregnant zookeepers into the feline building for fear they might contract the parasite, which several of the big cats carried. The parasite is known to damage human fetuses and cause miscarriages. It can be transferred to other animals as well, like rats. Weirdly, the parasite enters the rat's brain and changes the rat's behavior. Rats usually avoid cat urine, which is a good survival strategy. When they contract *Toxoplasma*, rats are attracted to cat urine, making it much easier for cats to prey upon them.

About 10 to 20 percent of Americans harbor the parasite, which can be absorbed through contact with litter boxes, drinking contaminated water, or eating undercooked meat. It was once thought that *Toxoplasma* hung out harmlessly in the human brain, but some scientists now believe that the parasite may actively change the connections among our neurons, altering personalities and even triggering mental illnesses like schizophrenia.

I'm not suggesting that we get rid of all cats. Far from it. I think cats are fabulous pets that give people great enjoyment and comfort. But I do believe that cats need to be controlled. We need to eradicate stray and feral cats. Birds are a vital element of our fragile ecosystems: They pollinate plants and trees, spread seeds, eat 400 million to 500 million tons of insects a year, reduce weeds, fertilize marine ecosystems such as coral reefs, and provide joy to the 60 million birders in North America (bird-watching is the second-most popular outdoor activity after gardening).

According to the Wildlife Society and the American Bird Conservancy, the average outdoor pet cat kills two animals a week.

You can help to solve this catastrophe. Spread the word about what cats are doing to the environment. If you come across a stray cat, take it to a shelter. If you own a cat, keep it inside. If you feel your cat deserves to be outside at times, supervise its activity so it doesn't kill birds. Leash laws are common for dogs, to keep them under control. Why not use leashes on cats too? If you can't do any of these things, I suggest you consider not getting a cat.

Chapter Six

Swarms

THE WESTERN HONEYBEE

(APIS MELLIFERA)

et's take a break and talk about a useful invasive species.

There are over 20,000 different species of bees buzzing around the world and 4,000 native bee species in the U.S. The bee you're probably most familiar with is the western honeybee. Guess what? The western honeybee is an invasive species, but it does more good than harm, so I don't consider it one of the "dirty thirty." It was brought to the U.S. in the early 1600s and is now found on every continent except Antarctica.

The western honeybee is thought to have originated in Africa or Asia. It first spread naturally into the Middle East and Europe, and was later introduced by colonists into North America, South America, Australia, New Zealand, and eastern Asia. When honeybees arrived in North America, Native Americans called them "white man's flies." Prior to the arrival of the honeybee, Native Americans didn't have words in their vocabularies for "wax" or "honey."

The honeybee has outcompeted many native bees, but as I said, their usefulness to humans and the environment has largely outweighed any problems the invasion has caused. Bees contribute an estimated $15 billion each year to the U.S. economy by pollinating our plants, trees, and flowers, including an astounding 85 percent of the crops that we eat. They are the only insect that directly provides a food eaten by humans. Honey not only tastes good, it also supplies us with several beneficial vitamins and minerals.

I could go on and on about the benefits of honeybees and why we need to preserve them, but that's not what this book is about. I'd better get back to other invasive insects— the ones that, to varying degrees, have been a disaster for us.

AFRICANIZED HONEYBEE

(APIS MELLIFERA SCUTELLATA LEPELETIER)

These so-called killer bees are actually hybrids, or "crosses," between the western honeybee and the East African lowland honeybee; they were created in the hope that the hybrid would produce higher yields of honey. The hybrids were brought to Brazil in 1957. Unfortunately, 26 swarms escaped during **quarantine** and the Africanized honeybee is now found throughout South America and as far north as the southern U.S.

Africanized bees' rapid expansion through South America, Central America, and Mexico created a media sensation in the 1970s. Prior to the bees' arrival in the United States, we were invaded by several terrible horror movies along the lines of *The Day of the Triffids*. I guess you'd call them "bee movies" instead of "B movies." *The Deadly Bees*, 1966; *The Savage Bees*, 1976; and *The Swarm*, 1978.

The real killer bees arrived in the U.S. in 1985 when they were discovered at an oil field in the San Joaquin Valley of California. It is thought this colony didn't fly overland but was hiding in a load of oil-drilling pipe shipped from South America.

The first permanent colonies arrived in Texas from Mexico in 1990 and spread to Arizona and other states. In 1994, a study of trapped swarms of our mild invasive honeybees near Tucson found that only 15 percent had hybridized with the African species. By 1997, this number had grown to 90 percent, which was worrisome.

Two more killer bee movies premiered in 2015, *Stung* and *Tsunambee*. I'm not sure what is worse, the films or the Africanized bees. I'm kidding—little Africanized bees are a big problem.

They are a lot more aggressive than our invasive western

honeybee. They've been known to chase people for a quarter of a mile and to sting ten times more often than our western honeybee. They have killed nearly a thousand people as well as horses and other animals.

SPONGY MOTH

(LYMANTRIA DISPAR)

The French artist, astronomer, and entomologist Étienne Léopold Trouvelot brought the spongy moth to the United States in the 1860s. He and his family lived in Medford, Massachusetts, just outside of Boston.

Silkworm moths were dying from various diseases in the U.S., and Étienne thought that the spongy moth might be a good substitute. So he imported several spongy moth eggs from Europe and started raising the larvae in the woods behind his house. Of course, the moths escaped. Then Étienne lost interest in entomology and concentrated on astronomy—while the spongy moths concentrated on devouring 300 species of trees and shrubs in the eastern U.S., making them one of the most destructive invasive species in the world.

From 1970 to 2010, spongy moths ate the foliage (leaves) of 80.4 million acres of trees and shrubs. This is known as **defoliation**. The worst year was 1981, when 12.9 million acres were defoliated. In 2010, 1,207,478 acres were defoliated. This problem has cost us millions of dollars in damage and has affected the reproductive success of our forest birds. Nests in defoliated areas have a higher predation rate because the nests are more exposed.

Spongy moths have few natural predators. Birds eat caterpillars, but they don't like the taste of spongy moth caterpillars. White-footed mice like eating spongy moth caterpillars, but white-footed mice aren't found in enough places or in enough numbers to control spongy moth outbreaks. There is a fungal pathogen that kills spongy moths, but it thrives only during very wet rainy seasons.

A biopesticide made from a deadly spongy moth virus called NPV has been used to control the moth population. Once the virus is introduced, it spreads through a moth colony like the common cold does among humans. NPV is specific to spongy moths, so it is safe to use in areas where native butterfly species occur. But NPV is difficult to produce and so is available only in very small quantities. As a result, people resort to traditional chemical sprays to combat the moth, but many of these sprays kill native species that live in spongy moth–infested areas.

FIRE ANT

(SOLENOPSIS INVICTA)

Getting stung by a fire ant is no fun. Believe me, I know. I've been bitten and stung by fire ants several times, and it hurts.

There are many different species of fire ants, but the invasive fire ant we have in the U.S. is the "red imported fire ant" or RIFA. Originally from South America, it was first noticed in Mobile, Alabama, in the 1930s. This introduction was thought to have come from an Argentinian cargo ship. There is little doubt that there have been many other invasion points because RIFA is found throughout the southern U.S. It is also found in Arizona, California, Hawaii, and several other countries around the world.

It is estimated that 30 to 60 percent of the people living in fire ant–infested areas of the U.S. are stung each year. Ouch. RIFA are aggressive and territorial. When disturbed they latch on to you with their powerful mandibles, and as if that isn't enough, they sting you with an alkaline venom mixed with toxic proteins. Some people have allergic reactions to the venom and die, but this is rare.

You might be wondering why people just don't stay away from fire ants. That's easier said than done when the ants are living in your yard. The slightest threat, like walking near their nest, can set off a painful RIFA attack. Once established, RIFA are very difficult to eradicate.

Insecticides work against RIFA, but as we've learned, some of these chemicals kill helpful native insects as well as harmful insects. Another problem is reinfestation. If you are successful in eradicating fire ants from your yard, there's a good chance a new ant colony will reinvade from someone else's yard.

RIFA do have natural predators. One of them is the tiny *Pseudacteon* fly, of which there are over 100 species. It is also known as the ant-decapitating fly. These flies reproduce by laying an egg in the thorax of a fire ant. When the egg hatches, the larvae migrate to the ant's head, feeding on muscle and nerve tissue. After about 2 weeks, the ant's head falls off, and the fly pupates in the detached head capsule. These flies have been introduced throughout the southern states in an effort to control the fire ant. This is known as **biocontrol**—introducing a harmless species to get rid of an invasive species.

Another predator is the carnivorous Venus flytrap, which lures ants with the sweet sap it produces. About 33 percent of the prey of the Venus flytrap are ants of various species. Unfortunately, the Venus flytrap is native only to North and South Carolina, and there aren't nearly enough of them to put out the flame of the red fire ant.

EMERALD ASH BORER

(AGRILUS PLANIPENNIS)

This little emerald ash borer is a picky eater. It only eats ash trees, millions and millions of them. It was first discovered in Detroit, Michigan, in 2002, although it may have reached the U.S. as early as the 1990s. It is thought to have arrived in wooden packing material from China, and is now found in 36 states.

There are 7 billion to 9 billion ash trees in the U.S. The ash is one of our most valuable trees, used for flooring, firewood, and baseball bats, among other things. The emerald ash borer lays its eggs in the bark of ash trees. When the eggs hatch, the larvae bore into the bark and feed on the inner wood of the tree for 1 or 2 years before they emerge as adults. This kills the tree from the inside out. Because the insects are borers, finding infestations is difficult. You can't get rid of something if you don't know where it is. When you find a dead ash tree, it's too late.

One of the techniques used to locate these infestations is **biological surveillance**. Researchers and volunteers follow parasitic wasps that lay their eggs in emerald ash borers. The wasps stun the beetles and carry them back to their ground burrows, where they are kept until the wasp eggs hatch and the larvae feed on the beetle. Researchers determine if there are emerald ash borers in the area by catching the wasps as they return to their burrows with their prey.

This seems like a painstaking way to find an infestation, but you can't very well check the bark of every ash tree in North America. This should give you some idea of how difficult it is to get rid of an invasive insect.

ASIAN CITRUS PSYLLID

(DIAPHORINA CITRI)

Do you like orange juice and lemonade? I do. Unfortunately, citrus trees are under bacterial attack by "yellow dragon disease," also known as "citrus greening," and "huanglongbing" (HLB). Citrus growers compare the disease to cancer. The vector for this deadly bacterium is an invasive insect, the size of a grain of rice, called the Asian citrus psyllid. It was first spotted in Florida in 2005. By 2011, HLB had reduced the citrus industry in Florida from 80 companies to 35, leaving trees, people, and livelihoods devastated. The disease is now found in Alabama, Arizona, California, Georgia, Hawaii, Louisiana, Mississippi, South Carolina, Texas, and Guam.

It's interesting to note that oranges are not a natural-growing fruit, but rather a cultivated hybrid: a cross between a non-pure mandarin and a hybrid pomelo. The orange has been around for thousands of years and probably originated in China. It was brought to Florida in 1565 when Pedro Menéndez de Avilés founded the colonial settlement of St. Augustine. Then Spanish missionaries brought orange trees to Arizona between 1707 and 1710. Franciscan monks brought the fruit to San Diego, California, in 1769. An orchard was planted at the San Gabriel Mission around 1804, and a commercial orchard was established in 1841 near present-day Los Angeles. In Louisiana, oranges were probably introduced by French explorers.

The Asian citrus psyllid infects citrus trees with HLB as it feeds on the sap. The bacteria starve the tree of nutrients so that its fruits are deformed, taste bitter, and drop before they ripen. When a tree is infected, it can easily pass the disease on to other trees. There is no cure for HLB. Infected trees are chopped down and burned. In Florida alone, HLB has cost billions of dollars in damage.

Up to 12,000 psyllids can accumulate on a single tree. Entire groves can become infected before the trees show any symptoms. Early detection and early response are the only way to stop the spread of HLB.

Spiders, lacewings, hoverflies, pirate bugs, and ladybugs prey upon psyllids, but they can't keep up with the psyllid reproduction cycle. Biocontrol has been used by introducing two species of wasps native to Taiwan, but again, they haven't been able to keep up with prolific psyllids. Insecticides kill psyllids, but they don't kill HLB. Once a tree is infected with HLB it is doomed and it will likely spread the disease to other citrus trees before it dies. Some orange growers believe that psyllids and HLB could cause the citrus industry to be eliminated in 10 to 15 years.

BROWN MARMORATED STINK BUGS (BMSB)

(HALYOMORPHA HALYS)

These stinky little insects invaded our farm a few years back and are still here. They spend the winter inside the exterior walls of our house and come out when the sun heats up the siding. Thousands of them. For us they are more a nuisance than noxious because we don't raise crops. We do have a few apple trees whose fruit my wife picks, peels, slices, and bakes into delicious apple pies. Our apples haven't been doing well since the stinkers moved in.

BMSB were first noticed in Allentown, Pennsylvania, in 1998. They are native to Asia, and it's thought they arrived from Japan or China on machinery or inside packing crates. By 2010, they had established themselves in several states and have now become a major orchard pest, costing the mid-Atlantic region $37 million in apple crop loss. They are found in over thirty states.

Stink bugs really do stink, especially when you squish them. Some people say they smell like the herb cilantro. Not to me. If cilantro smelled like a stink bug, I would never eat it again. People also say that a stink bug's body fluids are toxic and can irritate your skin and eyes, but it's never "bugged" me.

The terrible smell they emit comes from a gland in their abdomen. It's thought to be a defense mechanism to keep them from being eaten by birds or lizards. We don't have lizards on our farm, but I have seen birds eating them once or twice. I suspect stink bugs are not on the top of their treat list.

The stink bug's 6-to-8-month life cycle is predictable and observable. In fall when the weather starts to cool, they look for somewhere to spend the winter. When they find a suitable location, they invite their friends with a chemical signal, which is why you see them congregating on the outside of your house. Once they have found suitable shelter, they spend the winter in a state called **diapause,** a dormant state almost like hibernation. During diapause they don't eat, drink, or move much unless it warms up. This false start will bring them outside, but only temporarily. As soon as it gets cold again, they'll retreat into their shelter. When true spring arrives, they emerge from diapause permanently, eager to eat and breed.

A female stink bug can lay 400 eggs during her short life span. In the spring and summer she lays her eggs on the undersides of leaves. The eggs are light green when first laid, and gradually turn white. After a stink bug hatches, it takes 35 to 45 days for it to reach adulthood.

Stink bugs eat by poking their stylets (feeding tubes) into fruits, vegetables, and plants, extracting vital fluids the plant needs to survive. While harvesting the juices, stink bugs inject saliva into the plant, rotting the material underneath and making it vulnerable to disease.

Insecticides are not always effective against stink bugs, because they can bypass the toxin by feeding on the inner parts of fruits and vegetables where the insecticide doesn't reach.

What might save us from the invasive stink bug is another non-native insect from Japan and China called the samurai wasp (*Trissolcus japonicus*). It's a tiny stink bug warrior about the size of a sesame seed: You can't see it without the aid of a magnifying glass. No one knows how it came to the U.S. The strange thing is that entomologists were already growing and studying samurai wasps in laboratories, hoping to get government approval to sic them on the BMSB, when the wasp showed up on its own.

With plenty of BMSB egg masses to exploit, the samurai wasp has spread to several states, including Pennsylvania, New York, New Jersey, Maryland, Delaware, West Virginia, Virginia, Ohio, California, Michigan, Utah, Washington, and Oregon.

Female wasps seek out the egg masses of BMSB and

lay their own eggs inside the BMSB eggs. Instead of the BMSB eggs hatching BMSB nymphs, samurai wasps hatch. This just might be the magic switch that will rid us of the brown marmorated stink bug, saving my apples for apple pie.

MURDER HORNETS

(VESPA MANDARINIA)

At 1.5 to 2 inches long, the Northern Giant Hornet is the world's largest hornet—five times bigger than the honeybees you have in your garden. As the name implies, this hornet is native to Asia; it is also found in Russia. The nickname "murder hornet" is accurate, especially if you're a honeybee.

As I write this, murder hornets are not officially an invasive species in the U.S., but they have been spotted in northern Washington and southern British Columbia (Canada), which isn't good. No one knows how they got there, but it's clear that the two populations are not related. The hornets caught in Washington State underwent DNA testing and it was determined that they were from South Korea. The hornets captured in British Columbia were determined to be from Japan.

Murder hornets are normally solitary hunters, attacking bees one at a time, and are known to snatch them out of the air in midflight. Things change in the fall when murder hornets lay their eggs. They begin to hunt cooperatively, decimating entire beehives. A lone murder hornet cannot attack a beehive by itself, because the honeybees will swarm and kill it. To get around this, murder hornets send out scouts. When the scouts find a hive, they mark it with a **pheromone** (scent) and then wait for their nest mates to show up so they can all attack together. A single hornet can kill as many as 40 bees per minute using its large mandibles to quickly strike and decapitate them. The honeybee's sting is ineffective against murder hornets because they are heavily armored.

Once the bees are dead, the murder hornets drink the juices of their victims and dismember their bodies. The body parts are flown back to their nest and fed to their larvae.

The honeybees we have here are virtually defenseless against murder hornets, but Japanese honeybees have figured out a way to defeat them. They can detect the pheromone the murder hornet scout puts near their hive. With this warning, hundreds of bees gather near the entrance to the hive and set up a hornet trap. They swarm the attacking murder hornets, forming a "ball" around them, and vibrate their wings in the same way they heat their hive in cold conditions. This raises the temperature of the ball to 122 degrees and creates carbon dioxide, which kills the hornets.

In Japan, beekeepers keep murder hornets away from their hives with tennis rackets, swatting incoming murder hornets like they're tennis balls. Another method is to install an "entrance trap" on a managed hive: The trap allows the honeybees to come and go but is too small for murder hornets to squeeze through.

Unlike the honeybee, which can sting only once before it dies, a murder hornet can sting over and over again. People say their sting feels like getting stabbed by a red-hot nail. The stinger is long enough to pierce the gear beekeepers wear to protect them from honeybee stings. Murder hornets can also spray venom into people's eyes, causing severe damage. In Japan it's said that up to 50 people die from murder hornet stings every year, although the number is probably lower because victims may not know what kind of insect stung them. In 2013, it was reported that stings by northern giant hornets killed 41 people and injured more than 1,600 people in Shaanxi, China. Those who died were stung an average of 59 times while those who survived suffered, on average, only 28 stings.

In a few Japanese villages, people excavate murder hornet nests and eat the hornets. The larvae are considered a delicacy when fried. In the central Chūbu region, they are sometimes eaten as snacks or used as an ingredient in drinks. The grubs are often preserved in jars, pan-fried, or steamed with rice to make a savory dish called *hebo-gohan*. The adult hornets are fried on skewers, stinger and all, until their bodies become crunchy.

I hope we are successful in eradicating murder hornets in the U.S. If we fail, it will be a disaster for our invasive honeybees, food crops, native plants, and trees, and I can almost guarantee someone will make a horror film called *The Day of the Murder Hornets.*

Chapter Seven

Nibblers and Rooters

THE COPIOUS COYPU

THE COPIOUS COYPU

(MYOCASTOR COYPUS)

You probably know the coypu by its other Spanish name, *nutria*, meaning "otter," but it is not an otter and looks nothing like an otter. In Brazil it is known as *ratão-do-banhado*, or "swamp rat" in Portuguese, which is probably a more apt description because the nutria is in the rodent family. River otters and sea otters are in the *Mustelidae* family, which includes badgers, skunks, weasels, and wolverines.

The nutria was brought into the U.S. from South America as a get-rich-quick scheme in 1889 by people who thought nutria could be farmed for their fur (arguably the only beautiful thing about them). It didn't pan out, and farmers set their nutria free. Ground zero appears to have been Louisiana, where they spread quickly throughout the southeastern U.S., wreaking havoc on delicate wetlands. They are now found in 17 states, including Louisiana, Florida, Texas, Oklahoma, Arkansas, Tennessee, Georgia, Alabama, Mississippi, North Carolina, South Carolina, Delaware, Virginia, California, Washington, and Oregon, where I live. Louisiana alone has over 20 million nutrias gobbling up wetlands. No one knows how many nutria are now living in the U.S., but wherever they are found, they are causing serious damage to our ecosystems.

Nutria can weigh 9 to 20 pounds, sometimes more, and can eat up to 25 percent of their body weight every day. They are mostly vegetarian, but rather than just nibbling leaves, they eat entire plants, including the roots, making it less likely that the plants will grow back.

Female nutria can reproduce when they're 3 months old and can have 3 litters a year with up to 13 offspring each time, although the average litter is 4 to 9 pups. The mom nurses her babies like all mammals do, but the pups are able to eat plants within a few hours of birth.

The nutria's voracious appetite and constant digging behavior results in widespread erosion. This causes increased flooding, which in turn causes devasting land loss for native species.

England has managed to eradicate their nutria by intensive trapping, poisoning, and shooting. This has given land managers in the U.S. the hope that they might be able to eradicate them too. Unfortunately for Louisiana, with 20 million nutria, eradication isn't possible. All residents can hope for at this point is to control the invaders. Federal and state governments spend millions of dollars a year trying to stem the tide of this invasive rodent by aggressively hunting and trapping it.

HOGZILLA

(SUS SCROFA)

I like pigs. They are more intelligent and sensitive than they look. On animal intelligence charts they are usually listed at number two, just behind chimpanzees. From my experience with both species, this seems about right.

My first experience with feral pigs was on St. Vincent National Wildlife Refuge, where I was reintroducing red wolves into the wild. St. Vincent is a small barrier island in the Gulf of Mexico near Apalachicola, Florida. When we arrived at the dock with our crated wolves, the Florida Fish and Wildlife Conservation officials told us not to worry about bow hunters shooting our wolves. Confused, I asked them what they were talking about.

"You know, archers," someone answered, making a motion like they were shooting a bow and arrow.

"Are they hunting deer?" I asked. That was one of

the prey species on the little island we were counting on to keep the wolves fed.

"No, no, no . . . they're shooting pigs, feral pigs. There are hundreds of them here. They're rooting the island up."

"How long will the hunt last?"

"Just a couple of days by special permit. Don't worry about it. The wolves will be safe. The hunters will be long gone by the time you release them. We've cordoned off the release pens, so the hunters don't get too close."

I was more worried about the arrows reaching the wolves than I was about the hunters taking a peek at them, but I was happy the pigs were there because they would provide something else for the wolves to eat.

"How are the hunters getting around?" I asked.

"On foot and on mountain bikes."

No sooner had he said this, when a camo-clad hunter came stumbling out of the brush with a gutted pig strapped to his mountain bike.

"Those wolves you're letting loose are going to have good eatin' here," the hunter said. "That is, if they have a taste for pork."

It turned out the wolves did have a taste for pork, but the few they managed to take down and eat did not eradicate the feral pigs from St. Vincent Island.

The feral pig is a domestic pig that has escaped or has been intentionally set free. Pigs were introduced into the

U.S. in the 1500s by explorers. Seeding pigs on newly discovered islands and mainlands was common back then, so the explorers would have something to eat when they returned. In the 1600s, when the colonists arrived here, they brought domestic pigs to raise for food, some of which escaped. For the past 100 years, hunters have been releasing pigs into the wild as game animals.

A pig is a pig. Wild boars, domestic pigs, and feral pigs can all interbreed, and readily do so in the wild. There are an estimated 9 million feral pigs tearing up and eating native plants in the U.S. in 38 states, causing $2.5 billion in damage a year. Half of these feral pigs are found in Texas and the southern U.S. It used to be thought that feral pigs couldn't tolerate the cold, but over the centuries they have adapted to low temperatures by growing thick coats of hair. They are now found all the way up into Canada, primarily in Saskatchewan, Alberta, and Manitoba, where some pigs actually dig caves, or "pigloos," under the snow to stay warm. Pigs are omnivores. Their diet is mostly plant based, but they will eat just about anything they can find.

Feral pigs can carry at least thirty-two diseases, including bovine tuberculosis, brucellosis, and leptospirosis. Outbreaks of E. coli from the consumption of spinach and lettuce have been blamed on feral hogs defecating in farm fields. If a disease like African swine fever or hoof-and-mouth disease got into the feral pig population, they might easily spread it to our domestic animals, which could devastate the livestock industry.

A sow (female) feral pig can give birth when she is 6 months old. The average litter size is 6 piglets, but sows can give birth to as many as 12 piglets at a time. They can give birth twice a year. A feral pig can live as long as 14 years. This means a feral sow has the potential to produce hundreds of piglets in her lifetime. With 6 million feral pigs rooting around, and half of those sows, millions of new feral pigs are introduced into the wild every year. To keep up with this exploding pig population, wildlife managers estimate that they would have to remove 70 percent of the pigs in a given location every year to stop the population from increasing.

Wildlife managers are trying several techniques to stop the proliferation of feral pigs. Hunting is one option. In Texas, where feral pigs cause $400 million in crop damage every year, there is no limit on the hunting season for pigs. This means anyone can shoot a feral pig whenever they like, 365 days a year.

Another method used to eradicate feral pigs is to trap entire herds, or "sounders," as herds are called. Food is put out in a large catch pen to attract the pigs. The pen has a trapdoor that is left open on consecutive nights so the pigs get used to coming in and out of the pen to eat. The pen is monitored from a distance with game cameras and a special cell phone app. When the pen is full, the trapdoor can be closed remotely with the cell phone from miles away. Unfortunately, the trapping work is undermined if even one pregnant sow gets away. All she has to do is give birth in the wild and the cycle begins again.

Another technique is to poison the pigs, although it doesn't always work as pigs have a keen sense of smell and are suspicious of things they haven't encountered before. Poisoning is also controversial because it can kill non-targeted animals and can take a long time to work, which is inhumane. One poison that's used is warfarin, which is also used by humans as a blood thinner and to break up blood clots. In high levels, it is toxic to both animals and humans. Warfarin is commonly used to poison rats.

All these techniques are easier said than done, because feral pigs are intelligent and very good at staying alive.

A recent study found that mammal and bird communities are 26 percent less diverse in forests where feral pigs are present. The pigs outcompete native animals for food and ruin ecosystems with their foraging behavior. They have hastened the decline of nearly 300 native plant and animal species, many of which are already at risk. Feral pigs gorge on sea turtle nests from Florida to Texas, root out native milkweed vital to monarch butterflies and other pollinators, destroy the ground nests of birds, and pollute the breeding ponds of the endangered Houston toad.

Chapter Eight

Something Fishy Is Going On

With 71 percent of the earth's surface covered in water, it's not surprising that there are invasive fish devastating our aquatic ecosystems.

When I was a kid, we used to jump on our bikes with our fishing poles and ride over to the ponds along the Columbia River to fish for carp. They were fun to catch and beautiful to look at, but we never ate them. This was because the stagnant water where we caught them was polluted. The other reason was their weight. Carrying a 20-or 30-pound dead fish for 10 miles on a bike along with your pole and tackle box isn't easy. At the time I didn't know carp were invasive—in fact, I didn't know what the word *invasive* meant. To me, carp were as native as the starlings flying overhead and the nutria swimming in the pond.

CaRP

If you've seen a goldfish, you've seen a carp. Most carp species are native to Asia. There are: common carp, Amur carp, silver carp, largescale silver carp (from Vietnam), Asian grass carp, bighead carp, black carp, crucian carp, mud carp, and goldfish. Several of these species have invaded the U.S.

In China, carp have been cultivated as food for humans for over 1,000 years. They were initially brought to the U.S. for the same purpose. I've eaten carp in Thailand and Myanmar and it was delicious, but it hasn't caught on here.

The common carp, which is the carp I caught as a kid, has been in the U.S. for over 100 years. It's an invasive species, but it doesn't seem to be causing much of a problem in our lakes and rivers. The carp that are of most concern are bighead carp, black carp, grass carp, and silver carp. These carp were brought here in the 1970s to control weed and parasite growth in aquatic farms (fish farms). They managed to get into the 2,300-mile-long Mississippi River and its tributaries and are now found swimming and spawning in the wild as far north as Minnesota. Grass carp have been found in all the Great Lakes except for Lake Superior. The Mississippi River is a fish freeway with the potential of introducing Asian carp into 31 states. They are starving our native fish by outcompeting them for food, a concept you should be familiar with by now.

Black carp (*Mylopharyngodon piceus*) have molar-like teeth that crush and consume native mussels and snails, some of which are endangered. Grass carp (*Ctenopharyngodon idella*) are plant eaters. They can weigh as much as 100 pounds and can eat 40 percent of their body weight a day, which can completely alter aquatic food webs. Silver carp (*Hypophthalmichthys molitrix*) feed on the plankton needed by native larval fish and mussels.

Silver carp can lay up to 300,000 eggs a day. To put this into perspective, salmon can lay 17,000 eggs a day and native trout lay 400 to 3,000 eggs a day. It's easy to see how invasive carp are overwhelming our fish, aquatic plants, and other aquatic creatures.

Silver carp also cause "fish strikes." It turns out that the sound of boat engines causes silvercarp to leap 8 to 10 feet out of the water; when they do this, they often crash into boats and people. Getting hit by a 100-pound fish can cause serious injuries.

The best way to prevent an invasive species from establishing itself in a new area is to stop it from spreading. Control measures for the carp consist of putting up screened barriers and dams across rivers and streams so that carp can't cross them. Unfortunately, this can also stop native fish from migrating to their spawning grounds.

Another method used to control carp is electrofishing. Biologists put two electrodes into the water at high voltage.

This stuns the carp into **galvanotaxis**—uncontrolled muscular convulsions—causing the fish to float to the surface. At least two people are required for an effective electrofishing crew: one to operate the stunning machine, the other to scoop up the stunned fish with a dip net. In 2019, Kentucky declared a "War on Carp"; they used electrofishing to remove 5 million pounds of Asian carp from Lake Barkley and Kentucky Lake.

On the Tennessee and Illinois Rivers fish biologists are looking into putting the alligator gar, a predatory fish, into some of their waterways to control Asian carp. This prehistoric-looking predator can be 8 feet long and weigh hundreds of pounds.

Alligator gar are ambush hunters, meaning they lie in wait for their prey to swim by and then snap it up and swallow it. This might work for a juvenile carp swimming by, but a reproductive adult carp is too big for an alligator gar to swallow. Another problem is that alligator gars are opportunistic predators, which snatch waterfowl and small mammals as well as fish.

Asian carp are swimming and spawning their way north toward the Great Lakes. If they get there, it is feared they will ruin the Great Lakes $7 billion-a-year fishing industry.

In 2010 alone, the U.S. spent nearly $80 million in attempts to keep Asian carp out of the Great Lakes. The federal government is considering a $778 million plan to keep the carp away.

The carp problem is so extreme that even poisoning them has been considered, which isn't a good idea because poison can't tell the difference between a native fish and an invasive fish.

SNaKeHeaD

(CHaNNa aRGUS)

In 2002, an angler was fishing in a pond behind a strip mall in Crofton, Maryland. He pulled out an 18-inch fish with python-pattern scales and vicious teeth. He and his fishing partner were startled. They had never seen anything like it. They took a photograph of the fish and threw it back into the pond. When the Department of Natural Resources (DNR) received the photo, alarms went off. The angler had hooked a predatory northern snakehead.

The snakehead was eventually traced to a Maryland man who'd bought snakeheads in New York City and brought them to Maryland for his home aquarium. When they got too big, he released them into the pond.

To eliminate the snakeheads before they became

invasive, the DNR dumped a pesticide into the Crofton pond, killing all its fish. Six adult snakeheads were killed and more than 1,000 juveniles. Problem solved.

Not so fast. A couple of years later, snakeheads showed up in the 380-mile-long Potomac River not that far from the Crofton pond, but this turned out to been the result of a different release event. However, the Potomac River empties into Chesapeake Bay. Poisoning a pond is one thing, poisoning a river and a bay is an entirely different matter. You can't kill millions of native fish just to go after one invasive fish. These are the kinds of dilemmas fish biologists have to deal with every day. Snakeheads have also been spotted in California, Delaware, Georgia, Hawaii, Maine, Massachusetts, New York, Rhode Island, and Virginia.

The northern snakehead is native to China, Russia, North Korea, and South Korea. They can reproduce when they are 2 or 3 years old. A female can lay 100,000 eggs a year. The eggs are guarded by both parents until they hatch.

Unlike most fish, the northern snakehead has little sacs above its gills that function almost like lungs. When they surface, they suck air into the sacs, then draw oxygen from the stored air as they swim. The air sacs are handy for surviving in waters that are low in oxygen, and even give these fish the ability to survive out of water for a couple of days, as long as their skins don't dry out. This adaptation allows them to crawl on land for short distances to reach other bodies of water. Because of this ability and their ferocious appearance, snakeheads have been dubbed "Fishzilla" and "Frankenfish" by the news media. Like killer bees, the snakehead has spawned several films, including *Snakehead Terror*, *Frankenfish*, and *Swarm of the Snakehead*. You would think that films like this would help spread an awareness of the dangers of invasive species, but as fun as these films are to watch, perhaps just the opposite happens. Gross exaggeration of an invasive's ability to kill and eat people actually trivializes the harm they can cause. They have a ravenous appetite, but they don't eat us; instead, they take away the food we eat and completely disrupt our native ecosystems.

RED LIONFISH

(PTEROIS VOLITANS)

Let's leave our freshwater rivers, lakes, and streams and go snorkeling along the barrier reefs of North Carolina, Florida, and the Gulf Coast of Texas, where we are likely to see the red lionfish, which has been described by many fish biologists as one of the most aggressively invasive species on the planet.

Lionfish are native to the warm tropical waters of the Indian and South Pacific Oceans, nearly 10,000 miles away from where they are devouring fish off the shores of the southeastern U.S.

Years ago, I kept lionfish in my saltwater home aquarium, and I found them fascinating. When I started traveling and could no longer maintain my aquarium, I gave the fish away to friends who had saltwater aquariums of their own. Apparently, a lot of other aquarists who couldn't take care of their fish, or got tired of them, released them into the wild.

Lionfish were first seen along Florida coasts in the mid-1980s. (I know, poor Florida . . . again.) Since the fish were first detected their population has exploded in southeastern Atlantic marine waters, increasing as much as 700 percent in some areas. They now inhabit our reefs, shipwrecks, and other marine habitats. In some places, there are as many as 1,000 lionfish in a single acre.

In the western Atlantic, samples of lionfish stomach contents show that they consume more than 50 different marine species, including shrimp, juvenile grouper, and parrotfish, all species that humans also enjoy eating. A lionfish's stomach can expand up to 30 times its normal size after a meal. A study found that in as few as 5 weeks, lionfish can reduce the number of native fish on a reef by almost 80 percent.

It's not just their appetite that makes lionfish such frightening predators. It's the fact that native fish don't know a lionfish is a predator because it's new to their environment. They've never seen a lionfish before and don't know it's a threat. Scientists call this **prey naivete**. This is one of the reasons lionfish have been such successful invaders. Another reason for their success is how lionfish catch and eat their prey.

Having kept lionfish, I have some experience with how they eat. Believe me, it's quick. A lionfish uses a complex series of hunting tactics that no other fish uses. It floats innocently above its prey, and then in the blink of an eye it flares its fins, fires a jet of water from its mouth, unhinges its jaw, and swallows its prey whole. This happens much faster than I just described it. The victim simply vanishes. *Poof!* It's gone.

Lionfish have venomous fin rays, which is unusual for a tropical fish along the East Coast. For a human, getting nicked by a lionfish ray is painful, and there could be other reactions like nausea, vomiting, fever, breathing difficulties, convulsions, dizziness, headache, numbness, heartburn, diarrhea, and sweating, but you're probably not going to die, unless you're allergic to the venom.

Like all invasive species, lionfish are prolific. Females can reproduce when they are 1 year old and can release 30,000 unfertilized eggs every 4 days, which is about 2 million eggs per year. It's believed that the female's egg sacs contain a chemical that discourages other fish from eating the eggs.

Eradicating lionfish has been difficult. The only method that seems to work is to spear them one at a time. As they did with Burmese pythons, Florida biologists are holding lionfish derbies. Scuba divers gather at infested reefs where organizers offer prizes to the teams or individuals who catch the biggest, smallest, or most lionfish. The derbies do reduce the number of lionfish in a given area, at least temporarily, and are a good opportunity to educate people about the danger of releasing aquarium fish into the wild.

EUROPEAN GREEN CRAB

(CARCINUS MAENAS)

Another saltwater invader is the European green crab. Crabs are crustaceans, loosely related to spiders because they have exoskeletons, jointed legs, and are in the arthropod family. Oddly, the green crab's Latin name means "raving mad crab." They aren't crazy or angry, but they are causing a good deal of trouble for aquatic grasses and other crustaceans up and down our East and West Coasts. They are native to European and North African coasts as far as the Baltic Sea in the east, and Iceland and central Norway in the north. Although they are called green crabs their color varies from green to brown, gray, or red.

The first green crab in the United States was spotted in Massachusetts in 1817. They are found from South Carolina all the way up to Newfoundland. In 1998, green crabs were spotted in San Francisco Bay, and they are now found up and down the Pacific Coast, from Patagonia in South America to Washington State and south of Alaska.

A female green crab can produce up to 185,000 eggs annually. The larvae develop offshore in several stages before they become juvenile crabs and move closer to shore into the intertidal zone. Adult green crabs are only about 3.5 inches wide, but they are fierce little predators. One green crab can eat up to 40 small clams a day. They also eat scallops, mussels, oysters, fish, and other crabs, including their own kind. It is estimated that the green crab infestation costs East Coast commercial and recreational shellfisheries $20 million a year. On the West Coast, the cost is not nearly as high, but it is expected to increase exponentially as the green crab spreads.

Once the green crab establishes itself in coastal ecosystems, there is no effective way to eradicate it, but control measures are being taken. In 1995, residents of Edgartown, Massachusetts, held a green crab bounty program to protect local shellfish: 20,000 pounds of green crabs were caught and destroyed, but it didn't rid the area of the invasive crab. In 2014, a team of researchers used traps to remove most of the larger adult crabs from Seadrift Lagoon in San Francisco Bay, but instead of solving the problem, they created a bigger problem. It turns out that green crabs cannibalize their babies, which helps control the population, so reducing the number of adult crabs actually allowed the green crab population to grow.

The team adjusted their strategy to leave some adult green crabs present and managed to reduce the population in the lagoon by about 86 percent. Another method is to cover commercial shellfish with anti-crab nets, which is effective but also expensive.

Chapter Nine

The Day of the Triffids

There are thousands of invasive plant and tree species in the U.S. Unlike triffids, though, none of them arrived here on meteorites and none of them are going to uproot themselves and eat us, but they are causing a lot of trouble and costing us a lot of money.

Most of these invasive trees and plants were brought here as ornamentals for landscaping. People liked how they looked and planted them in their yards, and pretty soon the seeds spread everywhere: either blown by the wind or carried by birds, or from being stuck to the cuff of someone's pants or the soles of their shoes. The seeds germinated and grew into plants, which then spread more seeds across the country, eventually becoming invasives.

Most of the plants and trees we cultivate in our yards are not from North America. I have non-native trees and plants growing in my yard. Some of these are even invasive species, like our butterfly bushes, which we planted because feeding butterflies is good for our little patch of earth and does more good than harm.

Most of the fruits and vegetables that we cultivate and eat in the United States are non-native. However, they are not considered invasives, because they are useful to us and we are able to keep them under control. Carrots and spinach are originally from Iran. Peaches are from China. Apples are from Central Asia. Peanuts and tomatoes are from the Andes Mountains in South America. Oranges were originally found near the Himalayas. Potatoes have been cultivated in North America for thousands of years but are originally from Peru, where there are nearly 4,000 varieties. But for every useful plant we've brought into this country, there's another plant that's causing ecological damage. Collectively and officially these invasive plants are called **noxious weeds**.

These plants cost the U.S. economy $120 billion annually in lost crop and livestock production, control efforts, property value damage, and reduced export potential. In Oregon, where I live, the Department of Agriculture estimates that 21 invasive plant species reduce the combined income of all Oregonians by $83 million per year. These costs are passed on to consumers through higher prices for agricultural products. If farmers have to spend money to control noxious weeds, they are forced to raise the prices of their products. In effect, you and your family are paying for the removal of invasive plants.

KUDZU

(Pueraria Montana)

I first encountered kudzu in the South while driving around looking for places to reintroduce red wolves. It was hard not to notice the towering, impenetrable green vines engulfing trees, telephone poles, and derelict farmhouses. When I asked my colleagues from the Fish and Wildlife Service what this plant was, they answered, "Kudzu!" with disgust, as if they wanted to roll down the window and spit.

This noxious weed, also known as Japanese or Chinese arrow root, was first introduced to the U.S. at the 1876 World's Fair Centennial Exhibition in Philadelphia. The vine, native to Southeast Asia, was touted as a fast-growing ornamental and potential livestock food.

In the 1930s and 1940s, it was widely planted along roads and railway lines, and in farm fields to stop soil erosion. More than 70 million kudzu seedlings were grown in nurseries by the newly created Soil Conservation Service. Farmers were even paid to grow the invasive vine, as much as $8 per acre. When this planting spree was over, there were more than 1 million acres of kudzu growing in the South.

Kudzu is now found as far north as Canada. For a long time, it was thought that kudzu would engulf the entire southern U.S., but this hasn't actually happened. For one thing, kudzu doesn't grow well in dense forests, because there isn't enough sunlight for it to thrive. Yet it is still spreading at a pace of about 2,500 acres a year. Kudzu is considered an invasive because it grows to great heights as it reaches for the sun, preventing native plants from getting the sunlight they need to grow.

Needless to say, kudzu is no longer being planted to control erosion or as livestock feed. Instead, people are pulling it up from its roots in an attempt to stop it from spreading. Herbicides are also being used, but what might beat back kudzu to a manageable state is the invasive Japanese kudzu bug. It showed up in a garden near the Hartsfield-Jackson Atlanta International Airport about

10 years ago, probably by hitching a ride on an airplane. The little bug is now infesting vines throughout the South, slurping out the kudzu's vital juices. In places where it was once common to see kudzu, the bug-infested vines are so crippled they can't keep up with other roadside weeds.

CHEATGRASS

(BROMUS TECTORUM)

Cheatgrass is an apt name for this noxious weed because it "cheats" native plants from germinating. You've no doubt seen cheatgrass growing along roads and on disturbed soil even if you didn't know what it was. It looks like a miniature oat plant and is arguably the most invasive plant in the U.S.

Cheatgrass is native to Europe and East Asia. It was brought into Pennsylvania and New York in 1861, and is now found in all 50 states. This weed outcompetes native plants by germinating earlier and absorbing the water, soil nutrients, and sunlight other plants need to grow.

A single cheatgrass plant can shed enough seeds to grow 1,000 plants per square foot. These plants germinate in the winter, then die and dry out in the summer, creating serious fire hazards. Because cheatgrass bunches together, a spark from a campfire or a lightning strike can ignite thousands of acres of critical habitat in minutes. Once an area burns it becomes more susceptible to cheatgrass invasion, perpetuating the invasive cycle.

Areas that used to experience fire an average of once every 30 to 150 years may experience fires every 3 to 5 years after cheatgrass establishes itself.

So what's being done to stop cheatgrass's cheating ways?

Herbicides have been the primary method of getting rid of cheatgrass, but there are problems with this method. One problem is that herbicides kill native plants as well as invasive plants. Another is that herbicides kill only the cheatgrass *plants*, leaving the seeds in the soil to sprout the following year.

A recent innovation is to use soil **microbes** or **bacteria** that specifically attack cheatgrass root systems over time without harming native plants. The microbes don't kill cheatgrass outright. Instead, they inhibit cheatgrass growth, giving native seeds a chance to germinate, which stops cheatgrass from overwhelming a given area. The downside is that the bacteria take a long time to work—sometimes 1 or 2 years.

With more than 100 million acres of cheatgrass to eradicate, it's not likely that it will disappear anytime soon, but biocontrol could be an important tool for stopping the invasion.

ENGLISH IVY

(HEDERA HELIX L.)

English ivy was brought to the United States as early as 1727 by European colonists to remind them of their homeland. It was intended as a low-maintenance ground cover, but it quickly started engulfing native trees by blocking sunlight, which trees need to grow, and slowly choking them to death with their clinging vines. Its mildly toxic seeds are dispersed by birds. In the woods at the top of our driveway, we have English ivy, which is beginning to threaten some of our trees.

English ivy spreads quickly and thrives in both full sunlight and shade. The weight of the vines makes infested trees susceptible to blowing over during storms. English ivy has also been confirmed as a reservoir for bacterial leaf scorch, a harmful plant **pathogen** that affects a wide variety of native and ornamental trees such as elms, oaks, and maples.

Herbicides are used to eradicate English ivy, but as we know, this method can also kill native plants. The safest way to get rid of the weed is to pull it up by the roots and burn it. This is very labor-intensive because English ivy clings for its life to the ground, to buildings, and to the bark of trees.

Even though English ivy is considered a noxious weed, it continues to be sold and marketed as an ornamental plant in the United States.

PURPLE LOOSESTRIFE

(LYTHRUM SALICARIA)

Purple loosestrife is a beautiful plant, but don't be fooled. It's on the *loose* and it causes a great deal of *strife* for our native plants. It's been called "the purple plague" because of the damage it causes to wetlands. It has a strong taproot with up to 50 stems arising from its base, with several bunches of purple flowers. It tops out at about 6 feet high and can be 4 feet wide. A native of Eurasia, it was introduced to North America in the early 1800s in ships' ballast and as an ornamental. Ballast water allows ships to maintain stability and maneuverability during a voyage when they are not carrying cargo, not carrying heavy enough cargo, or when more stability is required due to rough seas. It is common for ballast to be contaminated with seeds, aquatic eggs, and microorganisms. Many invasive aquatic and plant species have been introduced around the world in this way.

Now found in every state except Florida, purple loosestrife is not banned everywhere. In states where it is still permitted, purple loosestrife continues to be promoted by horticulturists for its beauty as a landscape plant and for bees' forage. Thirteen states, including Minnesota, Illinois, Indiana, Ohio, Washington, and Wisconsin have passed legislation restricting or prohibiting purple loosestrife importation and distribution.

Purple loosestrife is a wetland plant found in fresh-water meadows and tidal and nontidal marshes, and along the banks of streams, rivers, ponds, reservoirs, and ditches. A mature plant produces over 2 million seeds annually. Most of the seeds are still able to germinate after 2 to 3 years in the water. Seeds are mostly dispersed by water, but wind, wildlife, livestock, vehicle tires, boats, and people also serve as seed vectors.

As purple loosestrife establishes itself and expands, it outcompetes and replaces native grasses, and other flow-ering plants that provide cover, food, and nesting sites for native wetland animals. It invades nearly 500,000 acres of wetland in the United States every year.

There are only four approved chemicals that can be used to manage purple loosestrife on delicate wetlands. For small infestations and isolated plants, hand pulling may be effective as long as you're careful not to disperse seeds. After pulling, the plants should be burned in order to destroy the seeds.

The non-native black-margined loosestrife beetle (*Galerucella calmariensis*) and the golden loosestrife bee-tle (*Galerucella pusilla*) are being used to fight loosestrife infestations. In the Great Lakes region, the National Sea Grant College Program has enlisted young people to raise and release *Galerucella* beetles to control this beautiful but invasive plant.

GIaNT HOGWeeD

(HeRaCLEuM MaNTeGaZZIaNUM)

In 1971, the rock band Genesis made this invasive plant famous with its song "The Return of the Giant Hogweed."

Around every river and canal their power is growing

[and later in the song]

They are invincible
They seem immune to all our herbicidal battering

The lyrics are a little inaccurate, but I always liked the song. I guess rockers are not necessarily ecologists.

Giant hogweed is a member of the carrot and parsnip family, but it's not safe to eat. It is native to the Caucasus region of Eurasia and was brought to Great Britain in the 1800s, then into the United States in the early 1900s, where it was planted in botanical and private gardens because of its size and impressive flowers. Like the fictional triffids, it escaped (although by seed dispersal and not on foot or slithering root) and spread into Connecticut, the District of Columbia, Illinois, Maine, Maryland, Massachusetts, Michigan, New York, Ohio, Oregon, Pennsylvania,

Washington, and Wisconsin, as well as the Canadian provinces of British Columbia, New Brunswick, Ontario, and Quebec.

The plant's scientific name (*Heracleum mantegazzianum*) comes from the name of the mythical Roman hero Hercules. It is far from heroic, but it is impressive to behold with its towering height (up to 15 feet), 5-foot-wide leaves, and 2.5-foot umbrella-shaped white flower heads. Each plant produces up to 100,000 half-inch-long, winged, flattened oval seeds in late summer, which accounts for its rapid spread. It outcompetes native plants by hogging soil nutrients and water, and by blocking sunlight so other plants can't grow. This, of course, is bad, but the primary reason it's considered an invasive species, or a federally designated noxious weed, is because it is poisonous to humans.

The sap from giant hogweed's 1-to-4-inch-diameter stems can give you **phytophotodermatitis**. This means your skin will burn if it makes contact with giant hogweed sap, and if the sap gets into your eye, it could blind you. Sunlight on the infected area makes the burning and blistering even worse. The only way to protect yourself from exposure is to wash the sap off right away with warm water and soap. Not easy to do in the woods. The other problem is that it can take twenty-four hours before you feel the effect of phytophotodermatitis on your skin, but by then it's too late: Your skin turns red and starts to itch, then lesions form, followed by large, fluid-filled blisters. The initial irritation will usually subside within a few days, but affected areas may remain hypersensitive to **ultra-violet** light for many years and re-eruptions of lesions and blisters may occur.

Manual removal can be dangerous for the people digging up the plants. Chemicals can be used, but this can put native plants at risk. Cutting hogweed down at ground level still leaves the root, which means the weed will grow up again. Cattle and hogs will eat giant hogweed and don't appear to be affected by the toxic sap, but eating the leaves, stems, and flowers doesn't destroy the root, which is the root of the problem because the giant will grow again.

Triclopyr herbicide is thought to be effective in killing hogweed without poisoning native plants and grasses, but the safest way to get rid of the plant is to dig it up by the roots and burn it so the seeds don't cause further infestations. This might have to be repeated over several growing seasons because it's difficult to dig up all of the roots the first time around.

Japanese Knotweed

(Fallopia Japonica)

In August 1850, the German botanist Philipp von Siebold sent a variety of plant specimens to the Royal Botanic Gardens at Kew in England. Among the plants was a rapidly growing perennial from Asia called Japanese knotweed. By "rapidly growing" I mean that Japanese knotweed can grow as much as 8 inches a day until it's 10 feet tall. It became popular in plant nurseries and spread throughout Great Britain. The knotweed in Great Britain are all clones of the original plant brought into Kew in 1850. This means a *single plant* managed to take over an entire country. Japanese knotweed has invaded several other countries, including North America, where it is found in 42 states and several Canadian provinces.

The knotweed's thick foliage blocks out sunlight so native plants can't grow. But the real problem with knotweed lies beneath the ground where its roots (rhizomes) snake out 40 feet wide and 10 feet deep, sucking up all the moisture and nutrients that native plants need to propagate. The rhizomes also release chemical compounds that can stop native plants from growing. Researchers have found knotweed root systems covering areas half the size of a football field.

Japanese knotweed is not dependent on seed dispersal to multiply. All that needs to happen is for a bit of its root (no bigger than your fingernail) to be moved somewhere else, which is how it spreads so quickly. Japanese knotweed is common along streams and rivers. If a stem or chunk of root falls into the water, it will propagate wherever it lands. Another way it's commonly moved is via truck. Builders and developers dig up knotweed because they don't want it on their building sites. Wherever the debris is dumped, knotweed will spring up. Those little bits of rhizome have a long shelf life: They can lie dormant for 20 years before sprouting.

It's no wonder people don't want Japanese knotweed anywhere near their homes. As knotweed seeks sunlight, it grows through concrete, house floors, walls, drainage systems, and foundations. Buildings and houses are often unsalable if Japanese knotweed is found on the property.

Eradicating Japanese knotweed is nearly impossible and very expensive. The United Kingdom spent $120 million to remove knotweed from the site of the 2012 London Olympic Games.

Closer to where I live, along the Sandy River in Oregon, the Nature Conservancy declared a 7-year war on knotweed. Two full-time employees and a squad of volunteers got permission from nearly 300 landowners to attack the noxious weed. They chopped it down, dug it up, sprayed it, and injected the thick stems with herbicide, year after year. They managed to kill 90 percent of the knotweed in the patches they treated, but this did not eradicate it.

Battles like this take place against knotweed every day, every year, all over the world. But help might be on the way in the form of a tiny psyllid from Japan called the *Aphalara itadori* (knotweed aphid). Unlike the citrus psyllid (mentioned earlier) that sucks the juices out of oranges, lemons, and other citrus plants, the knotweed aphid feeds exclusively on knotweed.

Introducing a non-native species for biocontrol is not

done without careful consideration. What if the new species causes more harm than good? We've learned from experience that introducing a non-native species to get rid of an invasive species doesn't always work and can have disastrous results. One example is when sugarcane planters released the small Indian mongoose (*Herpestes javanicus*) on several Hawaiian islands in 1883 to stop invasive rats from eating their crops. It didn't work out. Rats are nocturnal (active at night). Mongooses are diurnal (active during the day); therefore, rats are not on the menu when mongooses are out hunting. The mongooses found plenty of other things to eat, like ground-nesting-bird eggs, reptiles, amphibians, and turtle eggs. This has proved to be a huge problem for Hawaii's native wildlife.

Because of this and other biocontrol failures, governments are reluctant to approve non-native species in the fight against invasives. It took nearly 10 years for the U.S. Department of Agriculture to allow scientists to release the knotweed aphid into the wild. The first batch of insects were released in 2020. Researchers are waiting to see if they survive the winter. This biocontrol solution has not been without its critics. Beekeepers are not happy about eradicating knotweed because their bees feed on it. My opinion is that knocking out knotweed will allow native plants to come back, providing a variety of other flowers for bees to feed upon.

(HYDRILLA VERTICILLATA)

I had my first encounter with hydrilla around the time I saw *The Day of the Triffids*. It was in the goldfish (which are essentially little carp) aquarium I won at a carnival by tossing Ping-Pong balls at fishbowls. The balls were 3 for 25 cents. I probably tossed 100 balls before I managed to win a goldfish. When the man running the game handed me my fish, he stuffed a sprig of hydrilla into the bowl and said, "Green stuff. The fish like it."

The goldfish did like it, and the hydrilla liked the fishbowl because it grew like Jack's beanstalk. I had a hard time stopping the plant from smothering my goldfish. I kept the hydrilla under control by trimming it and throwing the cuttings into the garbage. I don't think the cuttings made their way into an unsuspecting pond, but you never know.

Hydrilla is native to Asia, Africa, and Australia. The first-known occurrence in the United States was in the 1950s, when an aquarium owner in Florida imported "Indian Star Vine" (another name for hydrilla) from Sri Lanka. He didn't like the looks of the plant, so he dumped it into a canal near Tampa Bay. From there it spread across the rest of the country and is now costing us millions of dollars a year to control.

Using herbicides has proved to be problematic.

Fluridone, a common and relatively safe aquatic herbicide, kills hydrilla. But after its first exposure, the plant becomes resistant to the poison. It's thought that hydrilla will become resistant to other herbicides as well.

Strangely, in 1996 hydrilla was indirectly responsible for the deaths of 29 bald eagles (our national bird) on the man-made DeGray Lake in Arkansas. Before the eagles died, they were seen flying into rock walls, hitting trees, and stumbling around on the ground like they were drunk. It took scientists over 20 years to figure out what happened to them.

Some of the other animals on the lake were exhibiting the same behavior as the eagles. One of those animals was a waterbird called a coot. The coots were feeding on hydrilla. In turn, the eagles fed on the sick coots and caught their fatal disease. Researchers took a microscopic look at the hydrilla in the lake and discovered a previously unknown blue-green algae (cyanobacteria) growing on it. On closer examination, they discovered that the new cyanobacteria had traces of the chemical element bromine on it. This deadly combination caused brain lesions in the birds. They named the bromine-tainted algae *Aetokthonos hydrillicola*, which is Latin for "eagle killer that grows on hydrilla."

Bromine is rarely found in fresh water, so how did it get into DeGray Lake? Scientists think it may have come from nearby coal plants, where bromine is used. Ironically, another theory is that the bromine came from herbicides used to kill the invasive hydrilla.

The only way to stop this deadly infection is to get rid of hydrilla. Using herbicides that have bromine is not an option. Scientists are now considering introducing sterilized invasive grass carp to eat the hydrilla, but the verdict is still out on this solution. Lab studies on whether the toxin affects fish have been contradictory. Bald eagles would certainly eat the carp. No one wants a repeat of this toxic cycle. It may turn out that the carp are safe. If that proves to be the case, we'll have an invasive species (hydrilla) being eradicated by another invasive species (grass carp) to save our national bird.

Chapter Ten

Mollusks

Slow moving, fast breeding, there are 81 invasive snails, mussels, clams, slugs, and other mollusks in the United States, costing us millions of dollars a year.

ZEBRA MUSSELS

(DREISSENA POLYMORPHA)

The little zebra mussel is causing big problems in the Great Lakes and other waterways across the country. Native to the southern lakes of Russia and the Ukraine, the first established population in North America was discovered in 1988 in Lake St. Clair, along our border with Canada. It's thought they were brought in by ships from overseas ports that were dumping ballast water into the lake.

The zebra mussel has spread into all the Great Lakes

and several major river systems, including the Ohio, Illinois, Mississippi, Mohawk, Hudson, Susquehanna, Tennessee, and Arkansas. Populations are now found in at least 23 states.

There are several reasons why this little mussel (the adult is about the size of a fingernail) has become a billion-dollar problem. One is its ability to reproduce. A female zebra mussel can release up to 1 million eggs a year. The eggs hatch into what are called **veligers**, which are microscopic larvae. The veligers drift with the current. Within 2 to 3 weeks, the veligers begin to "settle out" in the water under the weight of their developing shells, and they attach themselves to solid underwater surfaces. It takes approximately a year for the mussel to become capable of reproducing, and then the cycle begins anew.

Zebra mussels are sticky. They're armed with rootlike threads called **byssal threads** that grow along the hinge of their shells. This allows them to firmly attach themselves in clusters to rock, metal, wood, vinyl, glass, rubber, fiberglass, and the bodies of slow-moving animals like turtles and clams. They can close up their shells and live out of the water for as long as a week. When they attach to the hulls of recreational or commercial boats, they can easily be transported to new bodies of water.

Zebra mussels are filter feeders, which means they eat whatever phytoplankton (algae) drifts into their open shells. A single mussel is capable of filtering up to a quart of water a day. That is a lot of phytoplankton when you multiply it by the millions of mussels produced every year.

Native fish, clams, mussels, and other aquatic organisms are dependent on phytoplankton for their survival. Zebra mussels, by sheer volume, outcompete native animals for food and disrupt the aquatic food webs.

Because of their stickiness and clustering, zebra mussels are notorious "biofoulers." They clog the water intakes of municipal water supplies and hydroelectric dams. Researchers estimate that this has cost businesses and communities over $5 billion since the zebra mussel's initial invasion in 1988. The Great Lakes governing bodies in the U.S. and Canada spend $5 million a year on zebra mussel control. These costs are passed on to taxpayers, which means that we pay more for power and water because of this tiny invasive mussel.

But not all the news is bad. One beneficial side effect of the mussels' filtering activity is that the clarity of the Great Lakes has improved. You can see down for 30 feet in some of the lakes, compared to 6 inches 50 years ago. This clarity has caused some aquatic plants to thrive, which in turn has increased populations of smallmouth bass, yellow perch, and lake sturgeon.

We'll never get rid of the zebra mussel; all we can do is try to stop it from getting into other water systems. We can help with this by cleaning the hulls of our boats before we take them to another body of water, and by making sure shipping companies check ballast water for hitchhikers before dumping it into uncontaminated waters.

As I write this, there is a new vector for zebra mussels.

They have been discovered lurking in shipments of "moss balls" sold as aquarium accessories in pet shops across the country. Sales of moss balls have been reported in Alaska, California, Colorado, Florida, Georgia, Iowa, Massachusetts, Michigan, Montana, Nebraska, Nevada, New Mexico, North Dakota, Oklahoma, Tennessee, Vermont, Virginia, Washington, Wisconsin, Wyoming, and my state, Oregon. What would happen if an infected moss ball made it into one of these state's streams, rivers, or lakes?

Justin Bush, executive coordinator for the Washington Invasive Species Council, said, "This is one of the most alarming things I've been involved with in over a decade of working with invasive species." Rick Boatner, the invasive species wildlife integrity supervisor at the Oregon Department of Fish and Wildlife, commented, "A zebra mussel would be devastating to our environment if these ever got established in Oregon or the Pacific Northwest."

AFRICAN GIANT LAND SNAILS

(LISSACHATINA FULICA)

The African giant land snail is native to Kenya and Tanzania. I've been to both countries and saw many beautiful animals there, but not this behemoth. If I wanted to see one now, though, I wouldn't have to travel all the way to Africa because it is an invasive species in Florida and Hawaii.

These huge snails love subtropical climates but could spread into other states because they can hibernate during the winter. They are easy to spot because of their size (they weigh more than a pound and are about 8 inches long) and because they move so slowly.

The invasion started in 1966 when a ten-year-old boy smuggled 3 African giant land snails into Miami as pets. His grandmother later released them into her garden. Seven years later their population had exploded to 18,000, which cost the state of Florida more than $1 million and took 10 years to eradicate—or so it was thought. In 2011, giant snails reappeared. It's thought this second invasion was caused by the snails hitchhiking into the state attached to cargo or released by pet owners. They have no natural enemies in the U.S. Females can lay up to 1,200 eggs a year, and they can live 10 years. It is now illegal to import or sell African giant land snails in the United States.

They are known to feast upon over 500 different plants and are fond of eating stucco house siding for calcium to strengthen their shells. Perhaps worse, African giant land snails carry a parasite called "rat lungworm disease" that can transmit meningitis to people and pets. Meningitis is a serious illness affecting the spinal cord and brain, and it can lead to death if not treated. The snails get rat lungworm disease by eating rat poop. You can get it by eating or handling the snails.

Three years after the second invasion, Floridians managed to pick up and destroy 140,000 African giant land snails, but the giant invaders are still crawling around the state eating plants and houses.

Chapter Eleven

If You Can't Beat Them, Eat Them

We all have food biases. There are foods we like, foods we don't like, and foods we would never consider eating. Some of these biases are a matter of personal taste. I don't like cilantro, lima beans, or beets. They don't taste good to me no matter how they are prepared. Other people might relish a beet, cilantro, and lima bean salad. If there is such a thing, I shudder to think about it.

Some food biases are cultural, some are religious. Some people are vegetarian, vegan, freegan, or have no food taboos. Other people are poor and have little choice in what they eat. What's available to eat in one country may not be available in another country. For instance, I love Thai food, but Thai food in Thailand is different from Thai food in the United States. It's in fact better, because they use ingredients and spices that are not readily available here.

When my wife, Marie, and I travel overseas, we tour grocery stores to see what they have on the shelves, which is often different from what we have in the United States. We try to eat local cuisine when we can. Some of the unfamiliar food I've liked, and some I haven't. When I was in Myanmar years ago doing research for a book, the military officials running the country held a banquet for me and a friend. As I was sitting at the long table, a waiter brought me a plate with a duck head on it. I looked up and down the table. I was the only one with a duck head on my plate. The officials were all grinning and nodding at me like I had been given a duck head made out of solid gold.

My friend whispered, "You have to eat it. It's a big honor."

I like duck, but I prefer my duck not to look like a duck.

"How do I eat it?" I mumbled.

"Just pop it into your mouth, chew, and swallow."

I did, and I now consider duck head right up there with lima beans, beets, and cilantro. My point is that all food is fine to eat as long as you like it, and as long as it doesn't cause harm to you or to the ecosystem where it was raised or cultivated. I never make fun of people's culinary likes or dislikes. Food is food.

There's something relatively new in responsible environmental gastronomy (cultural food preparation) called **invasivorism**. The idea is that if we start eating invasive species, we can get rid of them, or at least control them.

It was first proposed by Joe Roman, a conservation biologist at the University of Vermont. He wrote an article for *Audubon* magazine titled "Eat the Invaders!" His premise was that if we can hunt native species to extinction, why not do the same thing with the invasives? He started the website EatTheInvaders.org. This was followed by another website, Invasivore.org, run by Matthew Barnes, an ecologist at Texas Tech University. Others followed, and there are now dozens of websites dedicated to the consumption of invasive species with recipes for all the animals in this book and many, many more.

Several chefs around the country have joined the invasivore movement by putting invasive species on their restaurant menus. For nearly 20 years, Louisiana's Department of Wildlife and Fisheries has been encouraging people to eat nutria by asking chefs to create tasty ways to prepare this rodent. In 2010, the National Oceanic and Atmospheric Administration (NOAA) launched an "Eat Lionfish" campaign. In 2011, Food & Water Watch hosted an invasive species banquet at the James Beard House in New York

City. Just south of where I live, the University of Oregon's Institute for Applied Ecology hosts an annual Invasive Species Cook-Off. To promote invasivorism, Whole Foods sells filets of Florida's invasive lionfish.

Pan-seared snakehead, smoke-pulled nutria, iguana tacos, poached Burmese python curry, kudzu jelly, marinated stink bugs . . . these are all legitimate recipes, but will eradication by mastication work? Probably not. But eating invasives could help control their expansion. The NOAA campaign to eat lionfish was adopted by the Catholic Church in Colombia, South America. In their sermons, the clergy suggested that their parishioners (84 percent of the population) eat lionfish on Fridays, Lent, and Easter. This resulted in a significant reduction of this invasive fish. In 2012, people in Illinois caught over 22,000 tons of carp and exported it to China, where it is commonly eaten, for $20 million. The lionfish are still off the coast of Colombia, and carp are still spawning in the rivers and lakes of Illinois. But there are fewer of those two fish than there were prior to putting them on a menu.

The ecologists promoting invasivorism are under no illusion that eating invasives will eradicate them, but they do believe that the movement is having a good effect by shining light on this difficult problem.

Some ecologists worry that invasivorism might work too well. Let's say nutria consumption becomes wildly popular with diners in the United States. Unlikely, I know, but if smoke-pulled nutria did become a popular dish, what's to stop people from breeding nutria to fulfill the demand? Remember, nutria were originally brought to this country so people could sell their fur.

My opinion is, if you get a chance to eat an invasive species, try it out. Who knows? You might like it. I can't end this chapter without including a recipe for my favorite invasive treat. I've eaten dozens of them over the years and I'm hoping my wife, Marie, will bake one when she reads this chapter.

PIE CRUST (IT'S ALL IN THE CRUST.)

Please note: Ask an adult to help while using the kitchen equipment required for this recipe.

1¾ CUPS FLOUR
¾ CUP CAKE FLOUR
½ TSP SALT
1 CUP BUTTER
1 EGG YOLK
1 TBS CIDER VINEGAR
COLD WATER

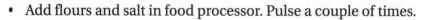

- Add flours and salt in food processor. Pulse a couple of times.
- Cut butter into 8 pieces, add to food processor, and pulse about 10 times.

- Lightly whip together egg yolk and vinegar with enough cold water to equal ½ cup. Gradually add liquid to dry ingredients in food processor while pulsing another 10 to 15 times, just enough so it comes off the sides of bowl.
- Divide in half, then cover in plastic wrap. Place in fridge for about 30 minutes. Roll out top and bottom crust for a 9-inch pie pan.

FILLING

6 CUPS BLACKBERRIES
¾ CUP SUGAR PLUS 2 TBS FOR SPRINKLING
¼ CUP FLOUR
½ TSP OF CINNAMON
1 TSP LEMON JUICE
1 EGG
2 TBS WATER

- Preheat oven to 450 degrees.
- Mix together: blackberries, sugar, flour, cinnamon, lemon juice. Let sit for 15 minutes. Mix and pour into the bottom crust in pie pan.
- Place the top crust over the filled bottom crust, then crimp and seal edges.
- Make an egg wash by whisking together egg and water in a small bowl. Brush a small amount on top pie crust. Sprinkle with extra sugar.

- Use a knife to gently cut slits in top to allow steam to escape.
- Bake 15 minutes at 450 degrees. Reduce oven temperature to 375 degrees and cook for another 60 minutes or until pie bubbles.
- Cover pie with foil or parchment if crust is browning too quickly.

Chapter Twelve

Are Humans an Invasive Species?

The best way to figure out the answer to this is to take another look at the nine points that turn a non-native species into an invasive species.

1. IT HAS TO GROW FASTER THAN THE NATIVE SPECIES SURROUNDING IT.

We are not particularly fast-growing, but we are long-lived compared to most animals on Earth. In the past 160 years, life expectancy in the United States has risen from 39.4 years in 1860 to 79.05 years in 2022.

2. IT HAS TO PRODUCE A LOT OF PROGENY (BABIES) QUICKLY.

A 9-month gestation period is not quick, but we make up for this in our large population, which grows exponentially every year. In 1810, the world population was 1 billion. Then 120 years later (1930), this doubled to 2 billion; then it reached 4.4 billion in 1975. Currently we have nearly 8 billion people living on Earth.

3. IT HAS TO DISPERSE (SPREAD) WIDELY.

We are everywhere now, including the Arctic and the Antarctic. This has been greatly helped by transportation technology. We can be anywhere in the world in a matter of hours or minutes.

4. IT HAS TO ALTER ITS GROWTH TO SUIT CURRENT CONDITIONS.

We are adaptable, resilient, and capable of altering our behavior in almost any way we choose.

5. IT HAS TO TOLERATE A WIDE RANGE OF ENVIRONMENTAL CONDITIONS.

We can tolerate most environmental conditions because we are able to clothe ourselves, make fire (heat), build shelters, invent and make tools (technology), and learn from other humans.

6. IT HAS TO HAVE THE ABILITY TO LIVE OFF A WIDE RANGE OF FOOD TYPES.

We are omnivores. We can eat just about anything that walks, swims, flies, slithers, or skitters.

7. IT HAS TO THRIVE NEAR HUMANS BECAUSE WE ARE ALMOST EVERYWHERE.

Humans are social creatures and generally get along with other humans.

8. IT HAS PROBABLY BEEN INVOLVED IN PRIOR SUCCESSFUL INVASIONS.

We have been exploring and colonizing the Earth for thousands of years.

9. IT CAUSES HARM TO EXISTING NATIVE ECOSYSTEMS.

We can and often do cause harm to ecosystems.

According to these criteria, there isn't much doubt that humans are an invasive species. Not only this, but we are also responsible for spreading thousands of other invasive species around the globe. What sets us apart is that we can *choose* between causing harm to ecosystems, or becoming custodians of ecosystems.

Chapter Thirteen

Biodiversity

There is no doubt that invasive species reduce *biodiversity*. I came across this word decades ago, as a new zookeeper reading about the animals I was caring for. I had no idea what biodiversity meant. I wasn't alone. The concept was relatively new back then. At the time, the most popular analogy was posed by ecologist Paul R. Ehrlich. It became known as the "the rivet popper hypothesis."

Imagine you are flying on an airplane (an enclosed ecosystem). All the parts on the airplane are joined by thousands of rivets. Each rivet represents a species. Let's say that passengers start popping rivets out of the airplane one rivet at a time. At first this doesn't affect the health of the airplane because there are many rivets/species holding the plane together (like the functioning of a healthy ecosystem). But if the rivet popping continues, one of those popped rivets will bring the airplane down and the ecosystem will crash, or more accurately, change. Usually, for the worse.

Ecological collapse is more complicated than this, but the analogy does explain how ecosystems can fail when animals, plants, and other organisms vanish. The simple truth is that the introduction of invasive species reduces the biodiversity that is vital to the health of our planet and everything living here.

Nature is always changing. Species come and go, but they are disappearing faster now than at any other time in human history.

According to the World Wildlife Fund, the world's populations of known mammals, birds, fish, and reptiles have dropped 60 percent since 1970. This alarming decline in biodiversity is the result of human activities like exploitation of natural resources, climate change due to our carbon fuel use, pollution, and the introduction of invasive species.

On our farm in Oregon, we are more interested in biodiversity then in how things look. About an acre of our property is landscaped, and I use the word *landscaped* loosely. Believe me, our place is never going to be on the front cover of a gardening magazine.

We have over 100 species of plants, shrubs, and trees. It looks nice, but the real purpose of the foliage is to attract and provide homes for native wildlife. We don't use herbicides or insecticides. We would rather pull a weed, or leave it where it is, than spray it.

We have over 30 species of birds with numerous areas for them to nest, and a variety of things for them to eat. We have deer, coyotes, foxes, skunks, weasels, raccoons, opossums, squirrels, rabbits, gophers, shrews, moles, rodents, tree frogs, garter snakes, and an occasional rubber boa (native to the Pacific Northwest).

We allow these creatures to live here because they are all part of biodiversity, just like we are. We like watching them. We try not to interfere with them too much, even if it's inconvenient for us. The only rule we have for the wildlife living here is that we don't allow them inside the house, which doesn't always work out.

I'm not an ecologist, but I try to think like one because it makes the observation of nature more interesting and meaningful. You, too, can think like an ecologist, and I hope you will. The thing that feeds my ecological mind is my insatiable curiosity.

If I don't know about an animal or a plant, I pull out my smartphone, or go to my computer, and learn something about it.

What animal or plant am I looking at? Why did it come to our farm? Is the species native or invasive? How does it interact with the other plants and animals in this ecosystem? How did it get here? What does the animal eat? What does the plant need to grow? What does the animal do when it's not eating? How does the weather affect it? When and where does it sleep? How does it reproduce? How many offspring does it have?

When do the offspring disperse? Is it passing through or will it stay on the farm? What effect will it have on the plants and animals that are already here?

Just like in my zoo days, curiosity still drives me. I learn something new every day.

Chapter Fourteen

Be Curious

Several years ago, one of my sisters-in-law put up bluebird nest boxes on our farm. In all the years we lived here, we had never seen a bluebird on our property. The adage "If you build it, they will come" came true, but it took five years until a pair of bluebirds finally moved in.

I became curious.

I found out that the bluebirds we had were western bluebirds (*Sialia mexicana*), and that they live year-round in the Willamette Valley where our farm is.

Most of the songbirds on our farm are primarily seed eaters. We've fed them supplemental seeds for decades. Our feeding regime is a bit selfish: Birds are more than capable of feeding themselves, but we feed them because we like watching them close up through our windows, although supplemental feeding does help birds during the winter and while they are nesting.

The downside to feeding seeds is wastage. Different

birds like different seeds. There is no such thing as a perfect birdseed mix. Birds pick through the seeds for their favorites and fling the rest aside. The discarded seeds land on the ground, which attracts rodents. Sometimes the rodents move into the house. I can't blame them. It's warm and safe inside, close to food (wasted seed), and we don't have a cat.

To get rid of the rodents, we stopped feeding the birds mixed seeds and switched to suet bricks, which cut down on wastage.

Bluebirds do not eat suet bricks. They eat insects and berries. We have plenty of those on the farm, but it's slim pickings in the winter. We wanted to entice the bluebirds to stay here because this is a safe place for them to live. Bluebird populations have plunged in recent years because of habitat destruction and invasive birds like starlings and sparrows dominating cavity nest sites.

The answer to keeping the bluebirds here was live mealworms. Bluebirds love them, but they are expensive. Years ago, when I worked at the zoo, we raised mealworms to feed to our birds and reptiles. Raising the worms costs virtually nothing, and once the mealworm farm is established, you have a lifetime supply of bluebird food. I set the farm up in my office under my desk. It was a lot more trouble than I remembered and it smelled bad.

I switched to dried bulk mealworms, even though several people claimed bluebirds would not eat them. This didn't make sense to me. Our dog would prefer steak or chicken, but she eats kibble and likes it. At the zoo we feed wolves kibble, and they do just fine on it, although I'm sure they would prefer elk venison.

Our bluebirds love dry mealworms. So do many of our other wild birds, and they don't waste them like they do with seed. I know this might seem like a lot of thought and trouble for a pair of bluebirds, but we invited them here by putting up the nest boxes. We aren't keeping them alive, we are just making it easier for them to stay here. We are trying to enhance our farm's biodiversity.

Within a few months, the bluebirds laid a clutch of eggs. Four chicks hatched, and we had 6 bluebirds eating dried mealworms. We watched the chicks grow up. They stayed through the summer and fall and then dispersed.

I just hope wherever they are now, there are some humans watching out for them. The parents stayed on the farm and have another batch of chicks that haven't left the nest box yet. I know they're in there because a couple of days ago I found broken shells on the ground beneath the box.

I end with this little story because I want you to know that you don't need to be an ecologist to preserve biodiversity.

All you need is curiosity and the willingness to lend a hand when the natural world needs help. We need to think about our actions and wonder what our decisions might mean to the plants and animals we depend upon.

After all, we are all in this together.

Glossary

AGRICULTURE: The growth of plants, animals, or fungi for human needs, including food, fuel, chemicals, and medicine.

BACTERIA: Unicellular microorganisms, which have cell walls but lack organelles and an organized nucleus, including some that can cause disease.

BIOCONTROL: The use of organisms or natural substances to prevent or reduce damage caused by animal pests, weeds, and pathogens.

BIODIVERSITY: All the different kinds of life found in one area, including animals, plants, fungi, and microorganisms. Each of these species and organisms works together in ecosystems, like an intricate web, to maintain balance and support life.

BIOLOGIST: A scientist involved in the study of living things.

BIOLOGICAL SURVEILLANCE: A systematic process that monitors the environment for bacteria, viruses, and other biological agents that cause disease; that detects disease in people, plants, or animals caused by those agents; and that tracks outbreaks of such disease.

BIPEDAL: An animal that walks on two legs.

BROOD: A group of related animals that emerges in a specific region in the same year. Depending on the animal type, the collective group is sometimes also known as a "year class." Verb: The act of guarding and/or incubating eggs.

BYSSAL THREADS: Strong, silky fibers that are made from proteins and are used by mussels and other bivalves to attach to rocks, pilings, or other substrates.

CARBON MONOXIDE: A poisonous gas that has no color or odor. It is given off by burning fuel (as from exhaust from cars or household heaters) and other products like dry ice and tobacco products. Prolonged exposure to this gas in an unvented environment prevents red blood cells from carrying enough oxygen for cells and tissues and can cause severe illness or death.

CLIMATE: The weather conditions that typically exist in one area, in general, or over a long period.

DIAPAUSE: A period of suspended development in an insect, other invertebrate, or mammal embryo, especially during unfavorable environmental conditions.

DEFOLIATION: To deprive a plant or a vegetated area of leaves.

ECOLOGY: A branch of biology that deals with the relations of organisms to one another and to their physical surroundings. A scientist who works in this field is called an "ecologist."

ENTOMOLOGIST: A biologist who specializes in the study of insects. A paleoentomologist studies ancient insects, mainly through their fossils.

GALVANOTAXIS: The movement of an organism or any of its parts in a particular direction in response to an electric current.

HERBIVORE: An animal that feeds mainly or only on plants.

INSECT: A type of arthropod that as an adult will have six segmented legs and three body parts: a head, thorax, and abdomen. There are hundreds of thousands of insects, which include bees, beetles, flies, and moths.

INVASIVE: An adjective that refers to something (such as an invasive species) that can invade an environment or alter an environment.

INVASIVORISM: The practice of eating invasive species as a means to control or eliminate their populations.

LARVAE: Immature insects that have a distinctly different form (body shape) than when they are adults. For instance, caterpillars are larval butterflies, and maggots are larval flies. (Sometimes this term is also used to describe a similar stage in the development of fish, frogs, and other animals.)

MICROBE: An organism that is too small to be seen without using a microscope, such as bacteria, archaea, and single cell eukaryotes (cells that have a nucleus, like an amoeba or a paramecium). Includes viruses.

MURMURATION: A phenomenon that results when hundreds, sometimes thousands, of starlings fly in swooping, intricately coordinated patterns through the sky.

NATIVE: Associated with a particular location; native plants and animals have been found in a particular location since recorded history began. These species also tend to have developed within a region, occurring there naturally (not because they were planted or moved there by people). Most are particularly well adapted to their environment.

NOXIOUS WEED: A plant considered harmful to the environment or animals, often the target of regulations governing attempts to control it.

OMNIVORE: An animal or person that eats food of both plant and animal origin.

PATHOGEN: A bacterium, virus, or other microorganism that can cause disease.

PEER REVIEW: The evaluation of scientific, academic, or professional work by others working in the same field.

PHEROMONE: A chemical substance produced and released into the environment by an animal, especially a mammal or an insect, that affects the behavior or physiology of others of its species.

POLLEN: Powdery grains released by the male parts of flowers and that can fertilize the female tissue. Pollinating insects, such as bees, pick up pollen and bring it back to their hive as food for the colony.

PHYTOPHOTODERMATITIS: An inflammatory eruption resulting from contact with light-sensitizing botanical substances.

PREDATOR: A creature that preys on other animals for most or all of its food. (Adjective: **predatory**.)

PREY NAIVETE: A phenomenon thought to be driven by the failure of a species to recognize an alien predator or invasive predator and respond accordingly.

QUARANTINE: A condition, time period, or place of isolation imposed upon people or animals that have arrived from elsewhere and might have been exposed to infectious or contagious disease.

SPECIES: A group of similar organisms capable of producing offspring that can survive and reproduce.

ULTRAVIOLET LIGHT: A type of electromagnetic radiation (also known as UV radiation) that causes summer tans—and sunburns. Too much exposure to UV radiation is damaging to living tissue.

VELIGERS: The final larval stage of certain mollusks, featuring two ciliated flaps for swimming and feeding.

VIRUS: Tiny infectious particles consisting of RNA or DNA surrounded by protein. Viruses can reproduce only by injecting their genetic material into the cells of living creatures. Although scientists frequently refer to viruses as alive or dead, in fact no virus is truly alive. A virus doesn't eat like animals do, or make its own food the way plants do. It must hijack the cellular machinery of a living cell in order to survive.

ZOONOSIS: A disease that can be transmitted to humans from animals.

Suggested Reading List

For readers who are curious about animals, ecology, and invasive species, here's a short list of books that scratched my itch and might scratch yours.

The Aliens Among Us: How Invasive Species Are Transforming the Planet—and Ourselves, by Leslie Anthony

A Walk in the Woods: Rediscovering America on the Appalachian Trail, by Bill Bryson

The Forgotten Pollinators, by Stephen L. Buchmann and Gary Paul Nabhan

Silent Spring, by Rachel Carson

The Death and Life of the Great Lakes, by Dan Egan

The Population Bomb, by Paul R. Ehrlich

A Better Planet: Forty Big Ideas for a Sustainable Future, by Daniel C. Esty

Invasive Plants: Guide to Identification and the Impacts and Control of Common North American Species, by Syl Ramsey Kaufman and Wallace Kaufman

The Sixth Extinction: An Unnatural History, by Elizabeth Kolbert

A Sand County Almanac, by Aldo Leopold

Biodiversity and Climate Change: Transforming the Biosphere, edited by Thomas E. Lovejoy and Lee Hannah

Cat Wars: The Devastating Consequences of a Cuddly Killer, by Peter P. Marra and Chris Santella

Limits to Growth: The 30-Year Update, by Donella Meadows, Dennis Meadows, and Jorgen Randers

The New Wild: Why Invasive Species Will Be Nature's Salvation, by Fred Pearce

The Song of the Dodo: Island Biogeography in an Age of Extinction, by David Quammen

Fuzz: When Nature Breaks the Law, by Mary Roach

The Beekeeper's Handbook, by Diana Sammataro and Alphonse Avitabile

Invasive Species: What Everyone Needs to Know, by Daniel Simberloff

Rats: Observations on the History & Habitat of the City's Most Unwanted Inhabitants, by Robert Sullivan

Beyond the War on Invasive Species: A Permaculture Approach to Ecosystem Restoration, by Orion Tao

Where Do Camels Belong?: Why Invasive Species Aren't All Bad, by Ken Thompson

Scratching Deeper

For those with a really bad itch, here's a selected list of scientific papers and articles that scratched my itch enough to write this book.

Papers and Articles

Ackerman, Daniel. "Invasive Giant Hogweed's Solar-Activated Sap Causes Blistering Skin Burns." *Scientific American*, July 2, 2018. scientificamerican.com/article/invasive-giant-hogweeds-solar-activated-sap-causes-blistering-skin-burns/

Ballew, N., N. Bacheler, G. Kellison, *et al.* "Invasive lionfish reduce native fish abundance on a regional scale." (2016). nature.com/articles/srep32169

Blossey, B., L. C. Skinner, J. Taylor. "Impact and management of purple loosestrife (*Lythrum salicaria*) in North America." *Biodiversity and Conservation* 10: 1787–1807, 2001. tsusinvasives.org/dotAsset/70f375ff-bd0d-471e-89c8-3faf1c2c65af.pdf

Borcyk, P., E. Fortner, M. N. Claunch, S. Johnson. "Florida's Introduced Reptiles: Green Iguana." Department of Wildlife Ecology and Conservation, UF/IFAS Extension. July 2021. edis.ifas.ufl.edu/publication/UW485

Chick, J. H., D. K. Gibson-Reinemer, L. Soeken-Gittinger, *et al.* "Invasive silver carp is empirically linked to declines of native sport fish in the Upper Mississippi River System." *Springer-Link* (2020). link.springer.com/article/10.1007/s10530-019 -02124-4

Doizy, A., E. Barter, J. Memmott, *et al.* "Impact of cyber-invasive species on a large ecological network." nature.com (2018). nature.com/articles /s41598-018-31423-4

Early, R., B. Bradley, J. Dukes, *et al.* "Global threats from invasive alien species in the twenty-first century and national response capacities." nature.com (2016). nature.com/articles/ncomms 12485

Fantle-Lepczyk, J. E., P. J. Haubrock, A. M. Kramer, R. N. Cuthbert, A. J. Turbelin, R. Crystal-Ornelas, C. Diagne, F. Courchamp. "Economic costs of biological invasions in the United States." *Science of the Total Environment*, volume 806, Part 3, 2022, 151318, ISSN 0048–9697. sciencedirect.com/science/article/pii /S0048969721063968

Fouts, K. L., N. C. Poudyal, R. Moore, J. Herrin, S. B. Wilde. "Informed stakeholder support for managing invasive *Hydrilla verticillata* linked to wildlife deaths in a Southeastern reservoir." *Lake and Reservoir Management* (2017), 33:3, 260–269, DOI: 10.1080/10402381.2017.1334017

Homan, H. J., R. J. Johnson, J. R. Thiele, G. M. Linz. "European Starlings. Wildlife Damage Management Technical Series." USDA, APHIS, WS National Wildlife Research Center. Fort Collins, Colorado. 26p. 2017. digitalcommons.unl.edu/cgi/viewcontent. cgi?article=1013&context=nwrcwdmts

Kadri, S., B. Harpur, R. Orsi, *et al.* "A variant reference data set for the Africanized honeybee, *Apis mellifera.*" nature.com (2016). nature.com/articles/sdata201697

Kuebbing, S., M. Nuñez. "Invasive non-native plants have a greater effect on neighbouring natives than other non-natives." nature.com (2016). nature.com/articles/nplants2016134

Little, B. "7 Species That Have Wreaked Havoc in The US: Feral Swine. Rodent of unusual size. And a python that swallowed three deer." *History Stories*, February 24, 2020. history.com/news/invasive-species-list-mammals-birds-aquatic

Loss, S. R., T. Will, P. P. Marra. "The impact of free-ranging domestic cats on wildlife of the United States." nature.com (2013). nature.com/articles/ncomms2380

Randall, B. "Invasive grasses are taking over the American West's sea of sagebrush." *ScienceNews*, December 6, 2021. sciencenews.org/article/invasive-grasses-spread-wildfire-plants

Risch, D. R., J. Ringma, M. R. Price. "The global impact of wild pigs (*Sus scrofa*) on terrestrial biodiversity." nature.com (2021). www.nature.com/articles/s41598-021-92691-1

Rogers, H., E. Buhle, J. HilleRisLambers, *et al.* "Effects of an invasive predator cascade to plants via mutualism disruption." nature.com (2017). nature.com/articles/ncomms14557

Ross, R. N. "The Invasive Rodents of Unusual Size." *Live Science*, January 13, 2020. livescience.com/nutria.html

Sangalang, J. "When cold weather strikes Florida, here's where you can likely find frozen iguanas." *Palm Beach Post*, January 28, 2022.

palmbeachpost.com/story/news/2022/01/28/florida-frozen
-iguanas-cold-weather-where-falling-trees/9244196002/

Sirsi, S., M. J. Marsh, M. R. J. Forstner. "Evaluating the effects of red
imported fire ants (*Solenopsis invicta*) on juvenile Houston Toads
(*Bufo* [=*Anaxyrus*] *houstonensis*) in Colorado County, TX." *PeerJ*,
February 10, 2020. ncbi.nlm.nih.gov/pmc/articles/PMC7017801/

University of Cincinnati. "Invasive species are taking over some
American forests: A plant survey finds dozens of nonnative invasive
species thriving in Ohio." *ScienceDaily*, June 17, 2022. sciencedaily
.com/releases/2022/06/220617162513.htm

University of Washington. "Brown tree snake could mean Guam will
lose more than its birds." *ScienceDaily,* August 10, 2008. sciencedaily
.com/releases/2008/08/080808090313.htm

US Department of Agriculture (USDA). "Invasive Species." fs.usda.gov
/managing-land/invasive-species

Vitousek, P. M., ed. "Severe mammal declines coincide with
proliferation of invasive Burmese pythons in Everglades National
Park." Stanford University, Stanford, CA, and approved December 21,
2011 (received for review September 26, 2011), January 30, 2012.
pnas.org/doi/10.1073/pnas.1115226109

The Wildlife Society. "Effects of an Invasive Species: Domestic Cats."
wildlife.org/wp-content/uploads/2017/05/FactSheet-FeralCats
_FINAL-1.pdf

Zaiko, A., D. Daunys, and S. Olenin. "Habitat engineering by the invasive
zebra mussel *Dreissena polymorpha* (Pallas) in a boreal coastal lagoon:
impact on biodiversity." *Journal of Biomedical Semantics,* 63, 85–94
(2009). hmr.biomedcentral.com/articles/10.1007/s10152-008-0135-6

Zhu, G., I. J. Gutierrez, C. Looney, D. W. Crowder. "Assessing the ecological niche and invasion potential of the Asian giant hornet," edited by Carl Folke. Royal Swedish Academy of Sciences, Stockholm, Sweden, September 22, 2022. pnas.org/doi/abs/10 .1073/pnas.2011441117

Acknowledgments

Books are written in solitude, but they are never written alone. I could not have written this book without the enthusiasm of my acquiring editor Julia Sooy, publisher Laura Godwin, production editor Lelia Mander, designer Julia Bianchi, publicist Kelsey Marrujo, production manager Jie Yang, and last, but far from least, my final editor, Mark Podesta, who brought this book over the finish line with great skill. I would also like to thank the Blake Street House, in Bentonville, Arkansas, for providing me the perfect place to write my books, and my literary agent, Elizabeth Bewley, from Sterling Lord Literistic, for keeping me calm. A huge shout-out to Gavin Scott for his beautiful illustrations that lightened up a very serious subject. And finally . . . my wife, Marie, who keeps our little ecosystem in perfect balance so I can write my books.